OREGON COAST

BARBARA TRICARICO

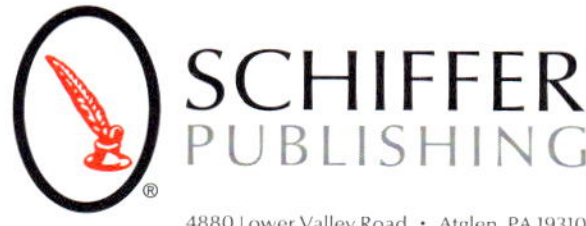

SCHIFFER PUBLISHING

4880 Lower Valley Road • Atglen, PA 19310

Other Schiffer Books by Barbara Tricarico:
Southern Oregon, ISBN 978-0-7643-5948-4
Oregon, ISBN 978-0-7643-5946-0
Central Oregon, ISBN 978-0-7643-5945-3
Ashland, Oregon, Day Trips, ISBN 978-0-7643-5014-6

Copyright © 2020 by Barbara Tricarico

Library of Congress Control Number: 2019947459

"Schiffer," "Schiffer Publishing, Ltd.," and the pen and inkwell logo are registered trademarks of Schiffer Publishing, Ltd.

Designed by Molly Shields
Cover photo: Brandon Herring
Back cover: center: Sue Stendebach; top right: George F. Peterson; middle right: Sue Newman; bottom right: Kate Geary

Type set in BentonSans/Cambria

ISBN: 978-0-7643-5947-7
Printed in China
5 4 3 2

Published by Schiffer Publishing, Ltd.
4880 Lower Valley Road
Atglen, PA 19310
Phone: (610) 593-1777; Fax: (610) 593-2002
E-mail: Info@schifferbooks.com
Web: www.schifferbooks.com

For our complete selection of fine books on this and related subjects, please visit our website at www.schifferbooks.com. You may also write for a free catalog.

Schiffer Publishing's titles are available at special discounts for bulk purchases for sales promotions or premiums. Special editions, including personalized covers, corporate imprints, and excerpts, can be created in large quantities for special needs. For more information, contact the publisher.

We are always looking for people to write books on new and related subjects. If you have an idea for a book, please contact us at proposals@schifferbooks.com.

INTRODUCTION

One of the prettiest drives you'll ever take is along Oregon's 363-mile coastline, considered one of the Seven Wonders of Oregon by Travel Oregon.

Weathered and rugged rock formations define each region along the Oregon coast. Bandon, with its world-class golf course looking out to the Pacific Ocean, is known for Face Rock. Cannon Beach is known for Haystack Rock. Cape Arago is home to the impressive Shore Acres State Park & Botanical Gardens. Barking sea lions draw visitors to Cape Arago or the Sea Lion Caves near Florence.

The mighty Rogue River empties into the ocean at Gold Beach. Here you can enjoy both river sports and ocean sports and eat local salmon or crab for dinner. Newport's draw is the 23-acre Oregon Coast Aquarium. The town of Charleston is a working fishing village. And *Architectural Digest* recently voted Manzanita the prettiest town in Oregon.

Brookings is a coastal town in a banana belt with temperate weather year-around. One of the longest dunes in the country is at the Oregon Dunes National Recreation Area. There's something for everyone along the Oregon Coast!

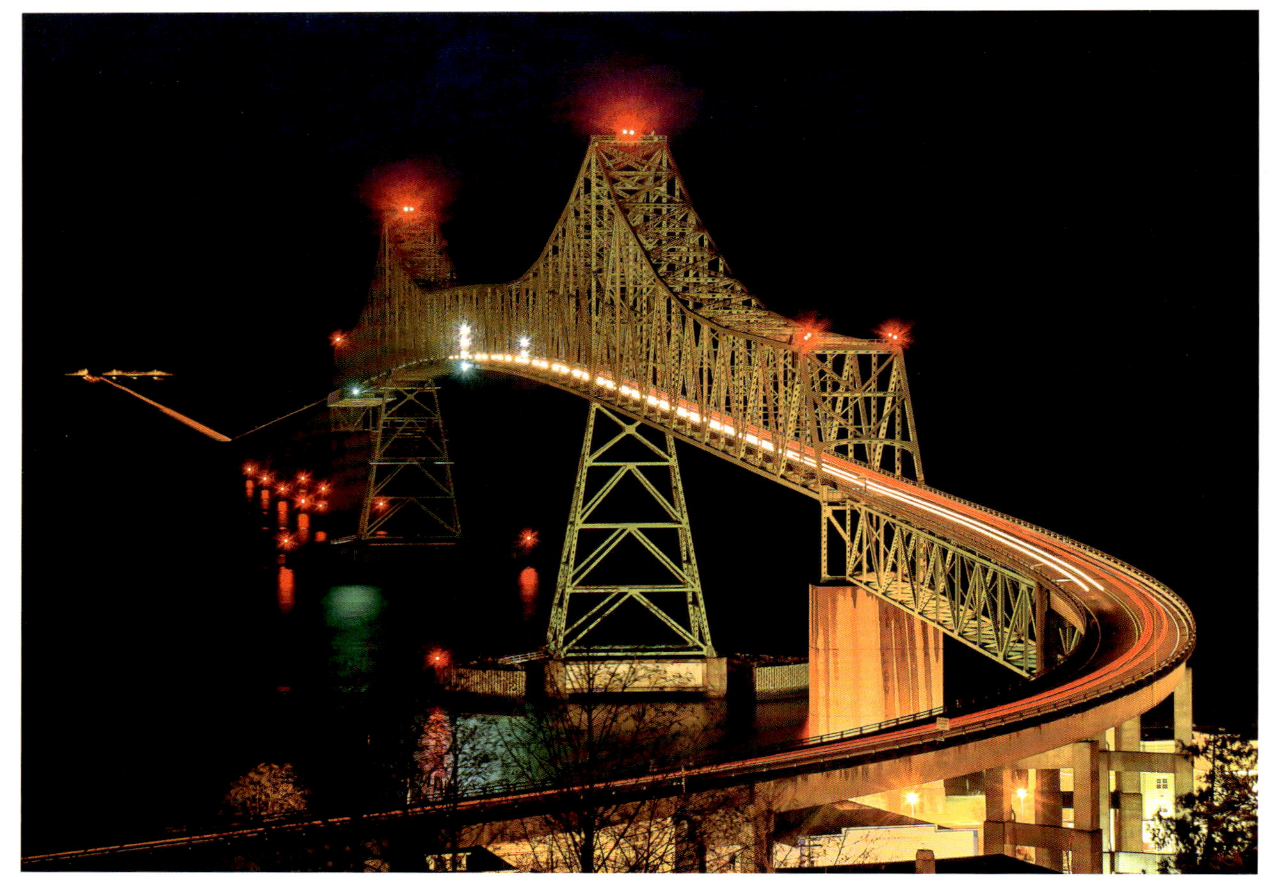

 Astoria-Megler Bridge is the longest continuous truss bridge in North America. *Photo by Clem Paslack.*

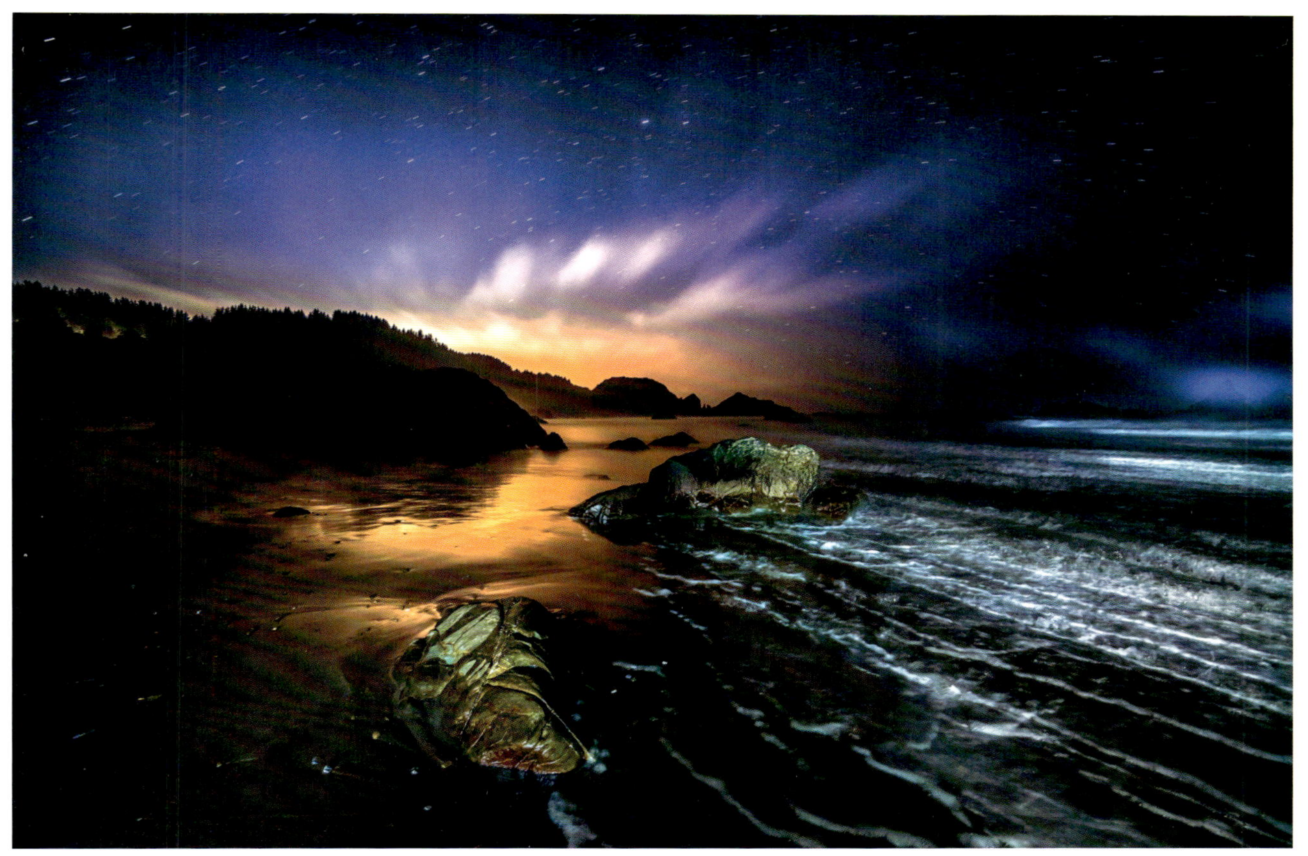

Coastline near Brookings. *Photo by Brandon Herring.*

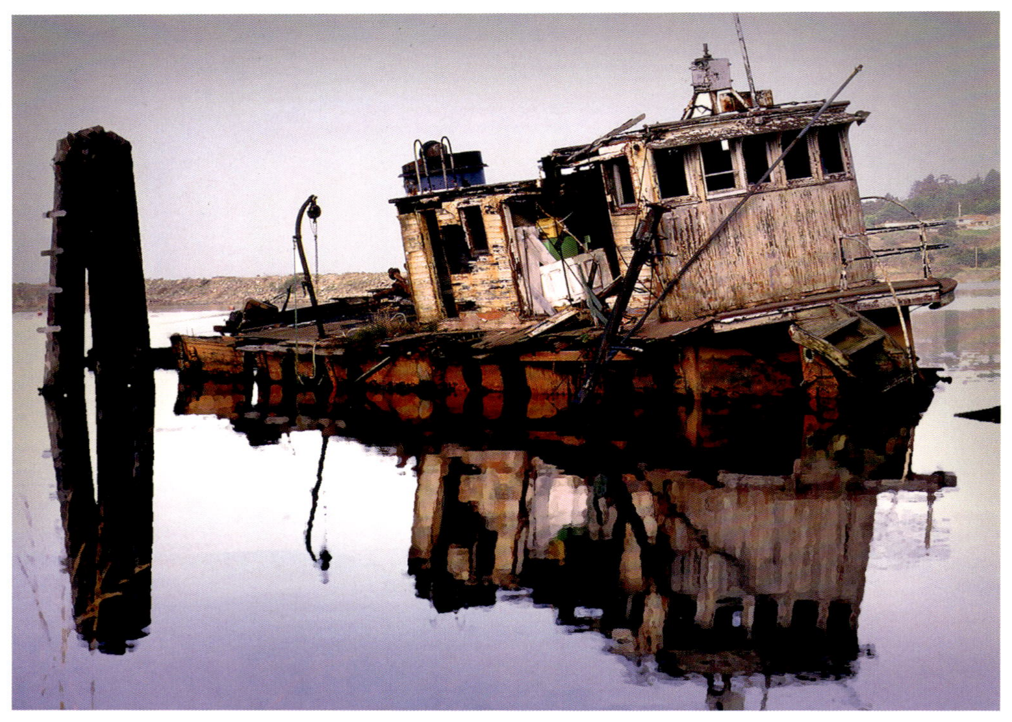

The *Mary D. Hume* was built in Gold Beach in 1881. The steamer also served as a whaling ship in Alaska and a tugboat. It sank in 1985 in the Rogue River, which empties into the Pacific Ocean. The *Mary D. Hume* is on the National Register of Historic Places. *Photo by John Kirk.*

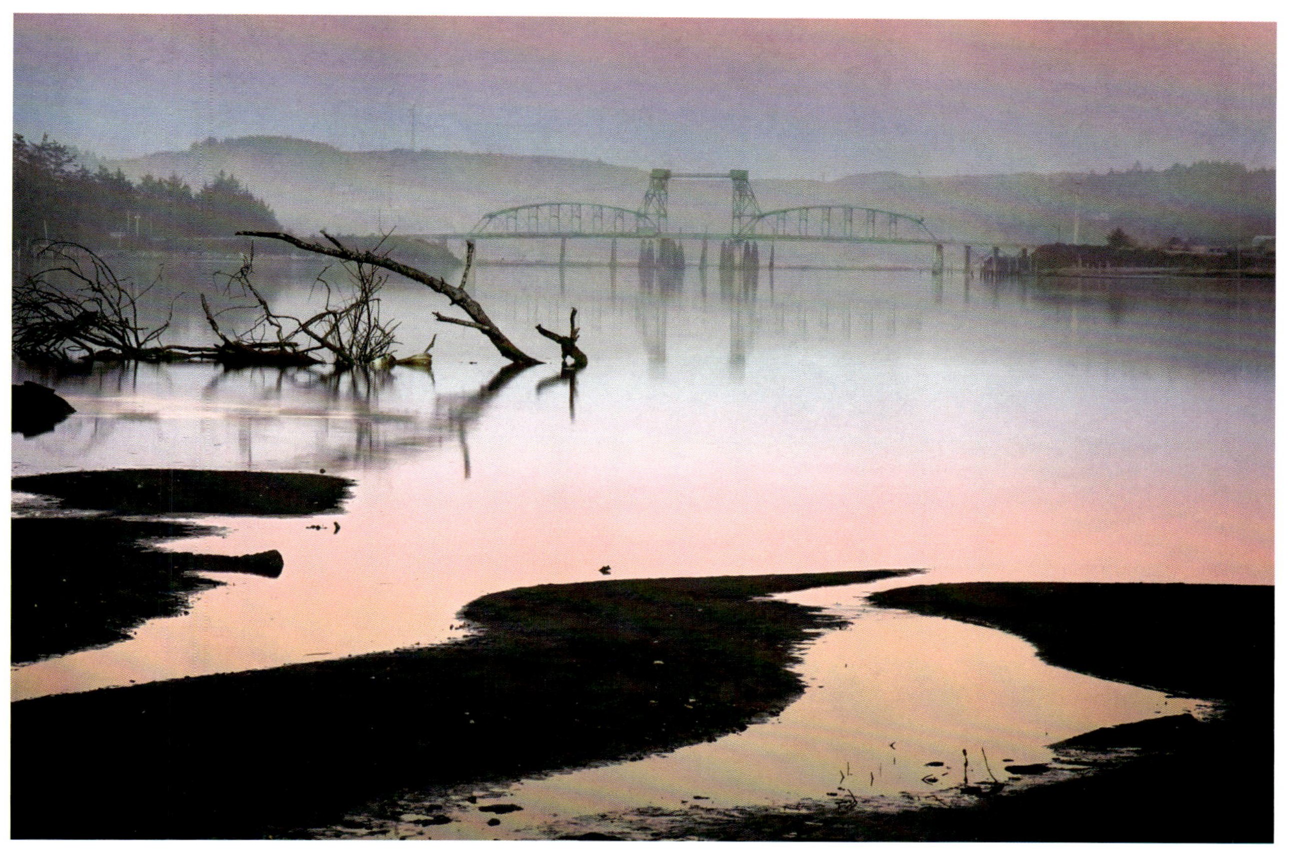

Bullards Bridge, Coquille River, opened in 1954. *Photo by John Kirk.*   7

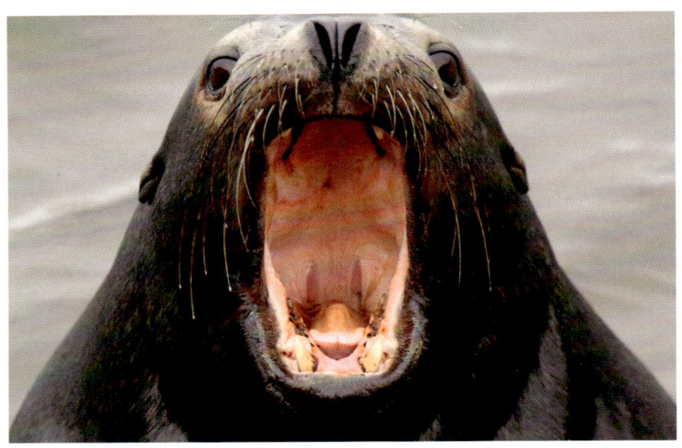

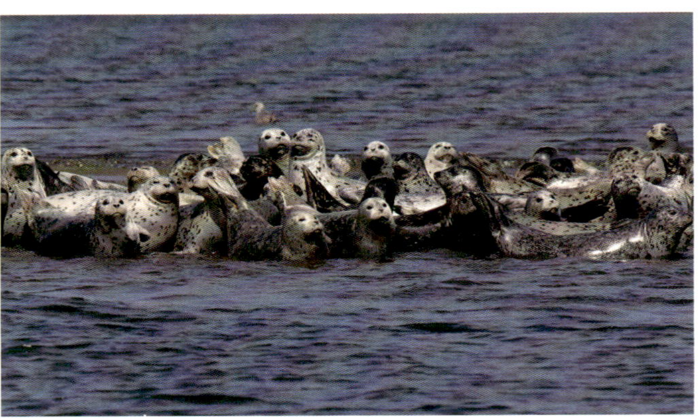

  Barking California sea lion in Gold Beach. *Photo by Dan Elster.* • Harbor seals at Gold Beach. *Photo by Dan Elster.*

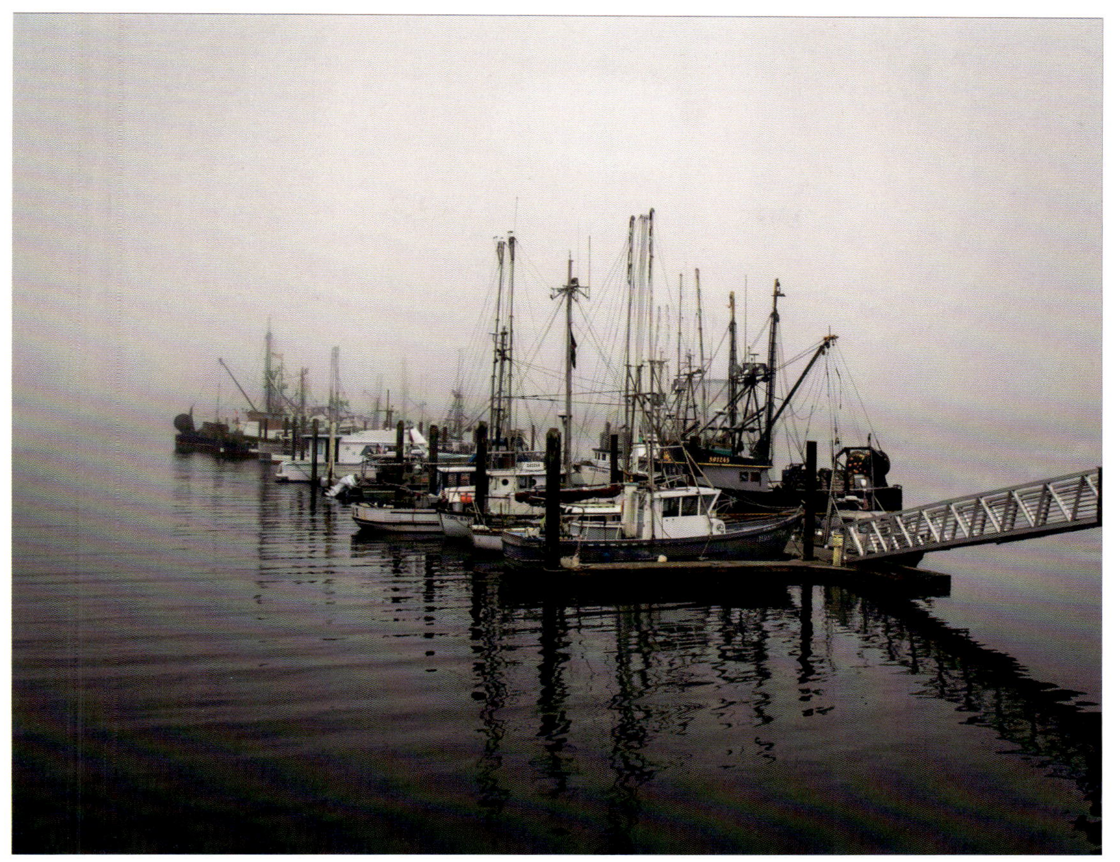

Charleston fog. *Photo by George F. Peterson.*   9

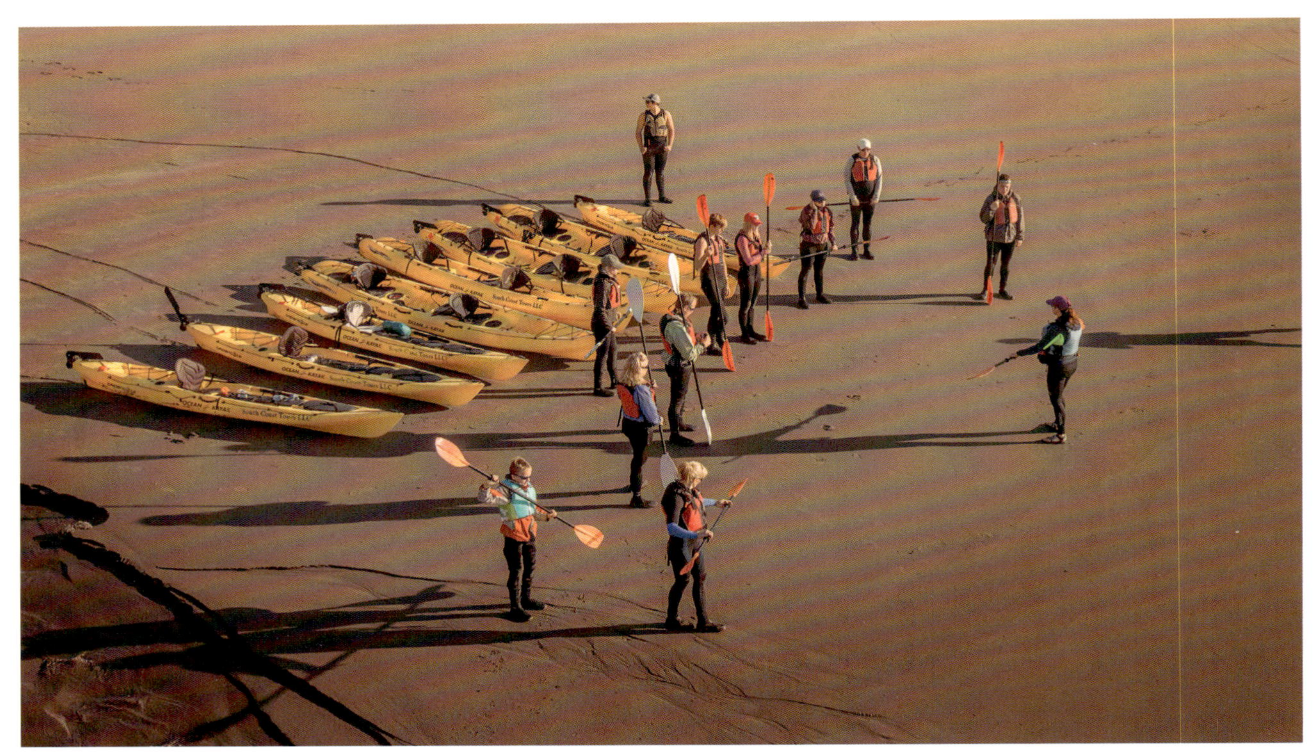

 Kayak instruction, Port Orford. *Photo by John Kirk.*

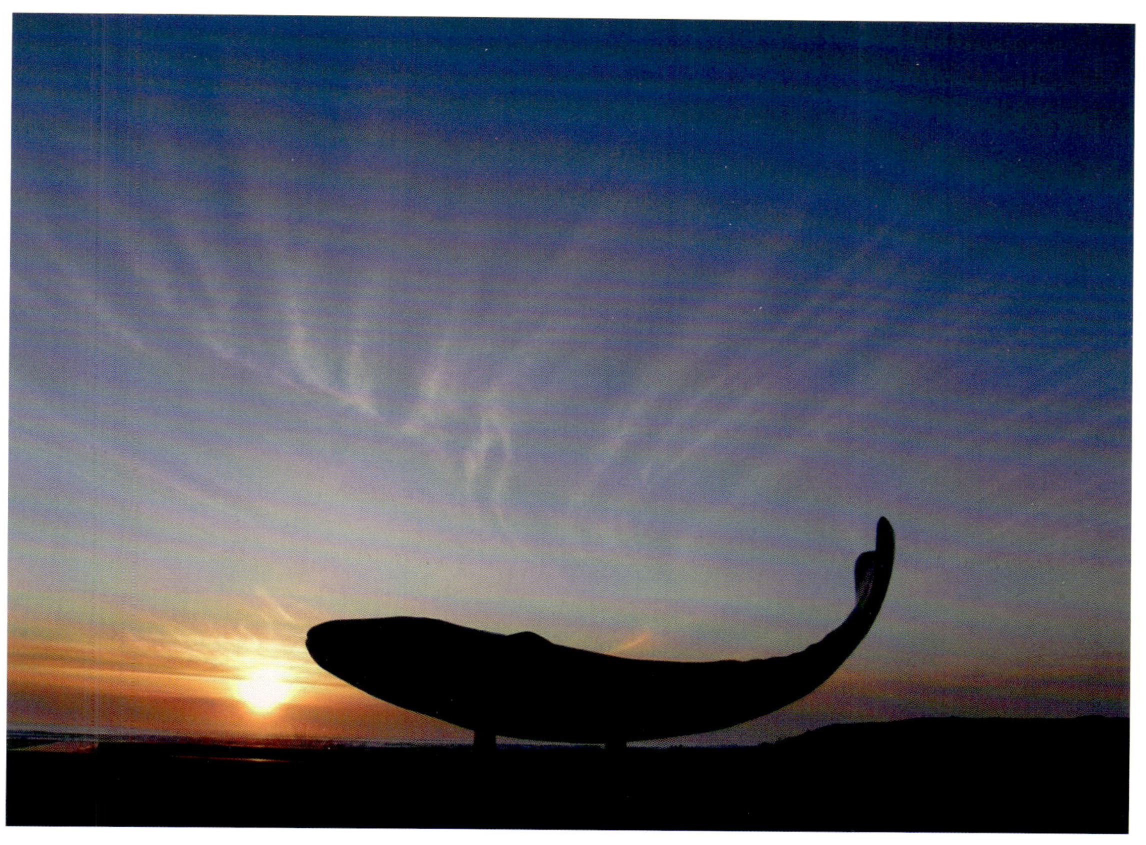

Sunset at Whale Park, Cannon Beach. *Whale* is a sculpture that commemorates the discovery of a whale skeleton in January 1806 by the Lewis and Clark expedition. *Photo by Charles Hillestad.*

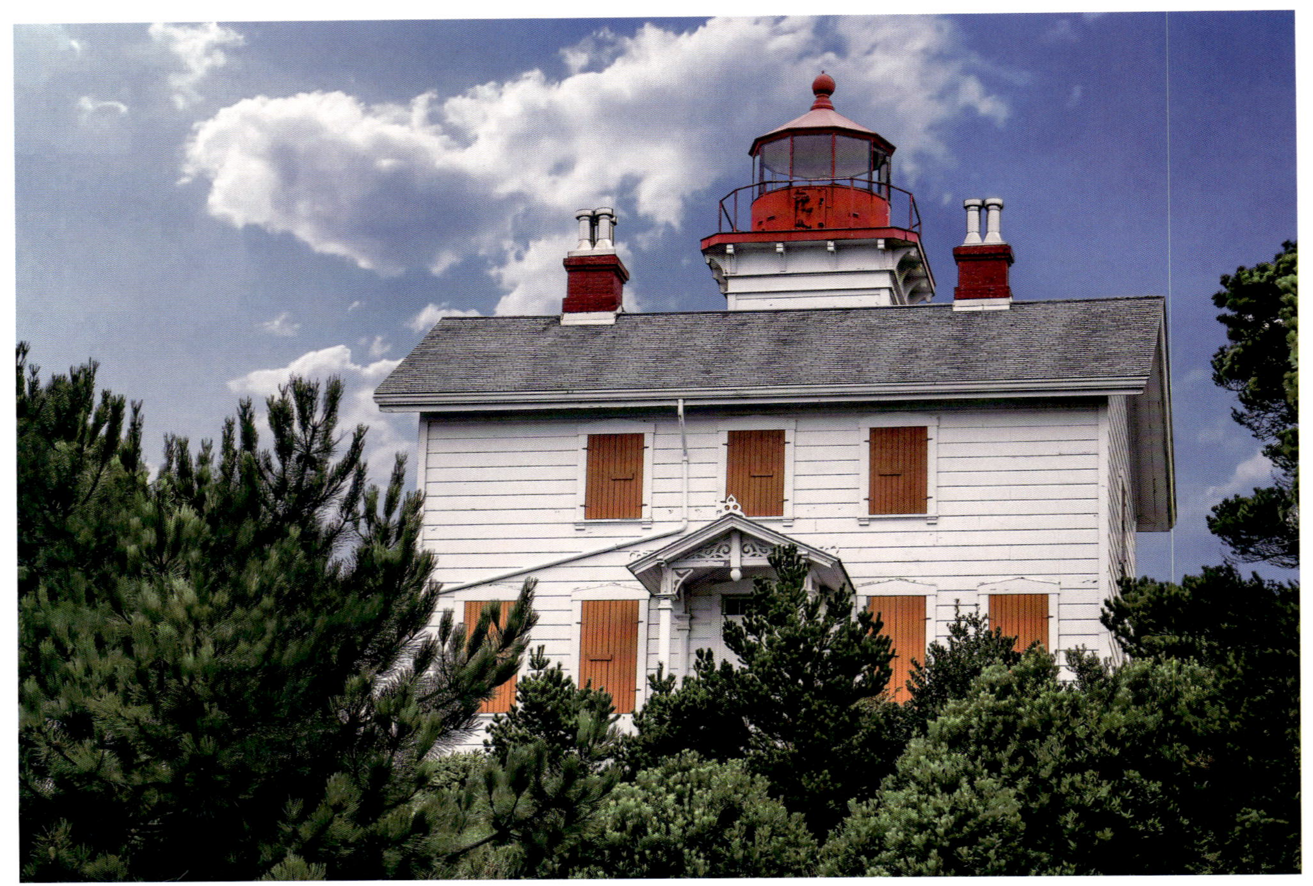

 Yaquina Bay Lighthouse, Newport, is believed to be the oldest structure in Newport, built in 1871. *Photo by Terry Fisher.*

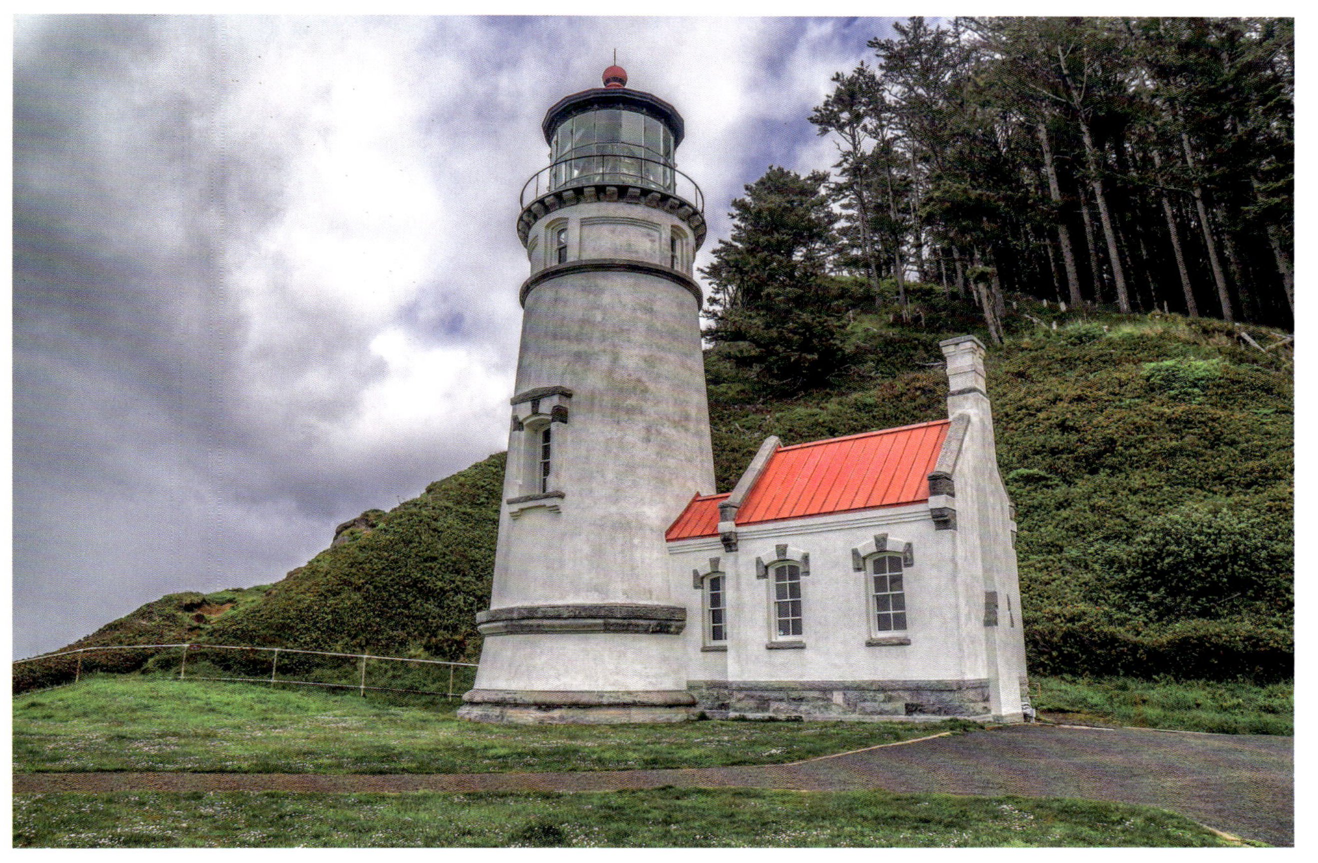

Heceta Head Lighthouse, built in 1894, is located between Florence and Yachats. It stands 56 feet tall and is the strongest light on the Oregon coast. *Photo by Terry Fisher.*

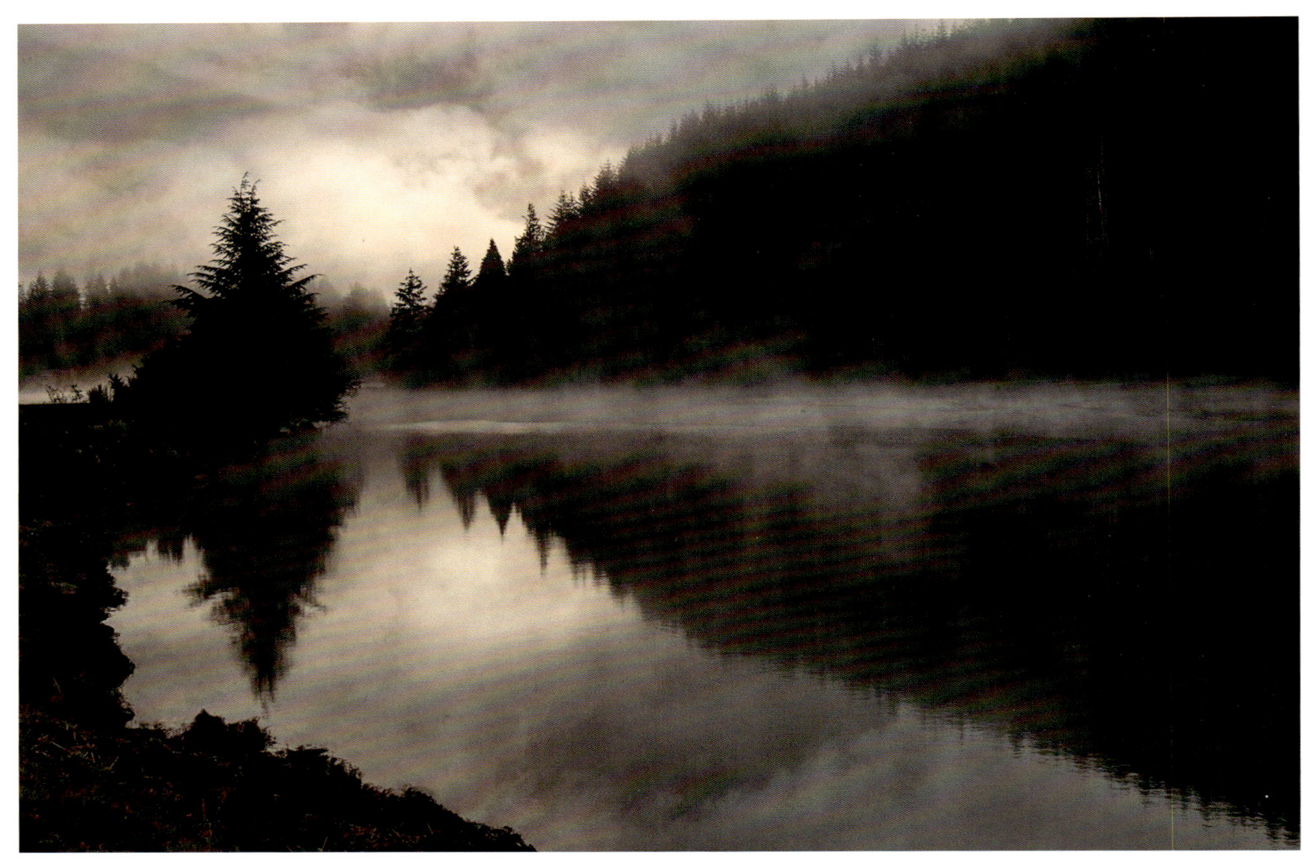

14   Coos Bay fog. *Photo by David Lorenz Winston.*

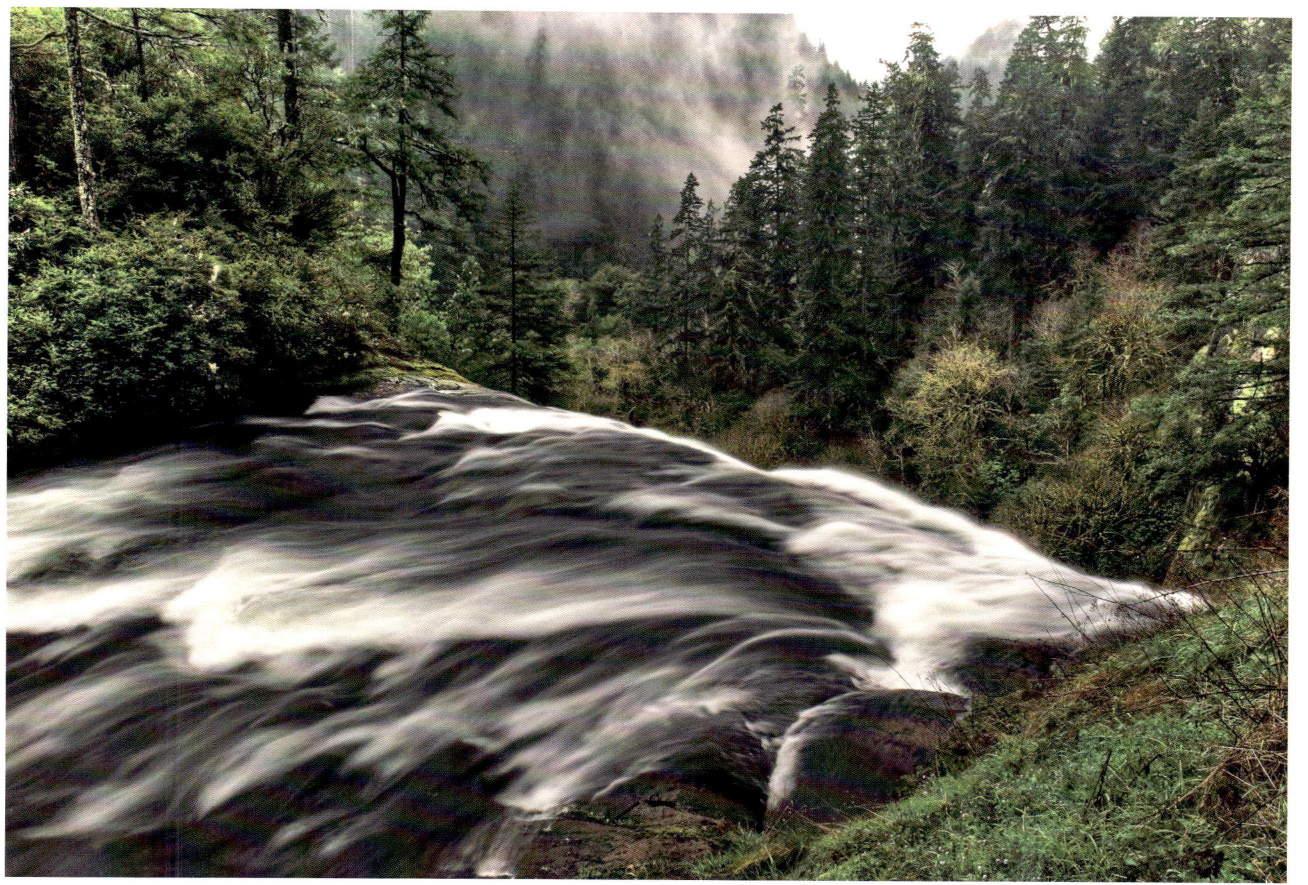

Golden Falls. *Photo by Jay Newman.*   15

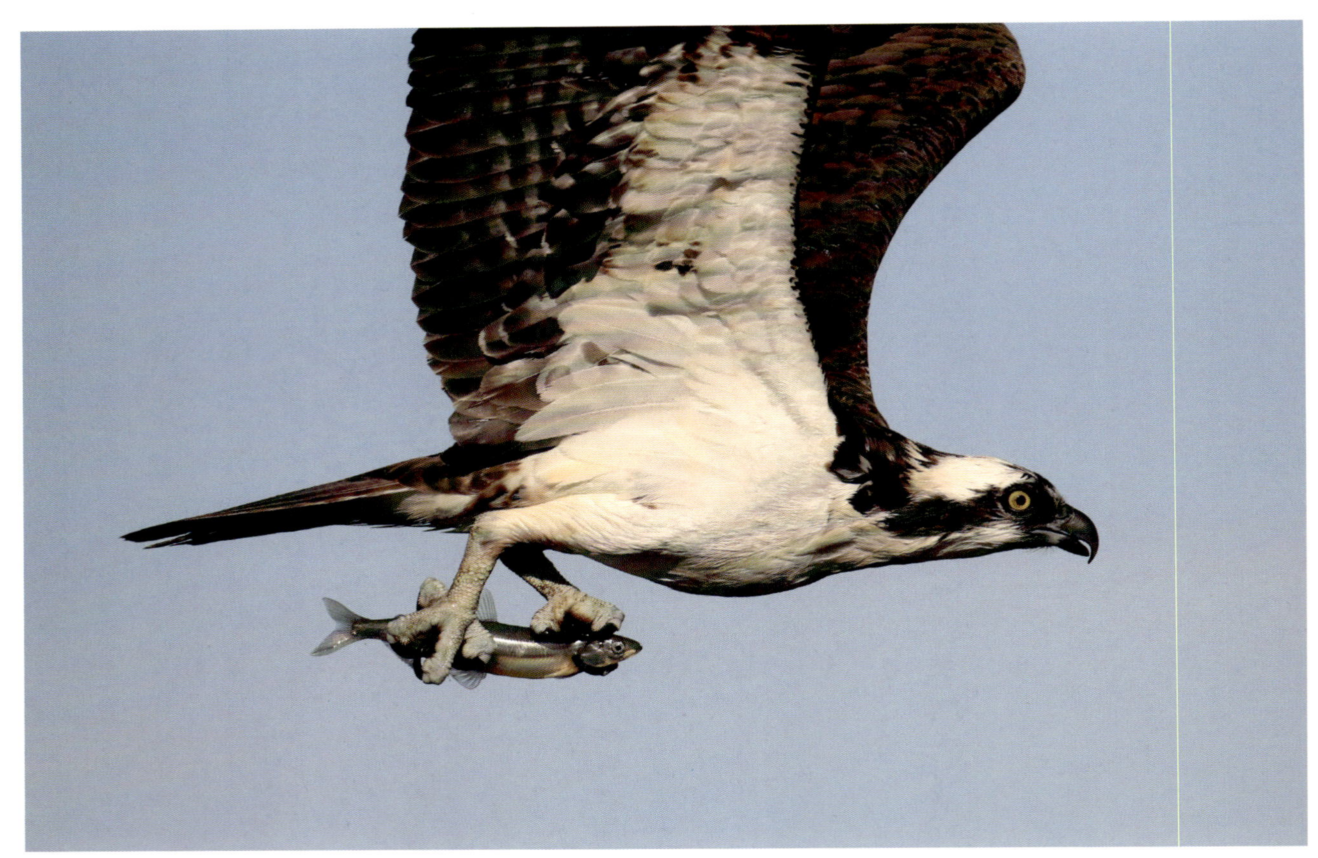

16   Osprey and its catch, Gold Beach. *Photo by Dan Elster.*

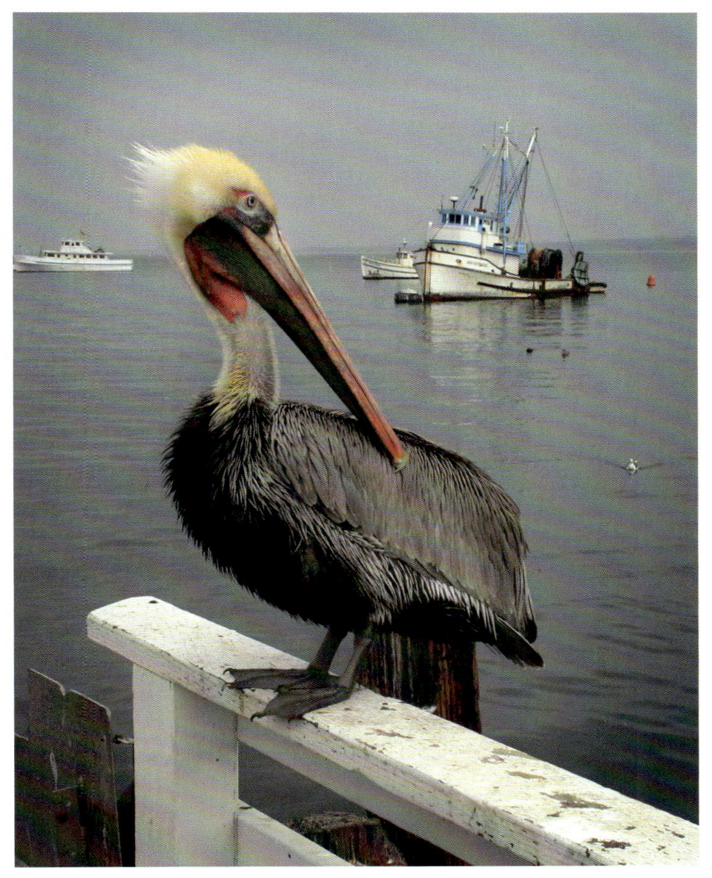

Pelican in the harbor. *Photo by John Kirk.*

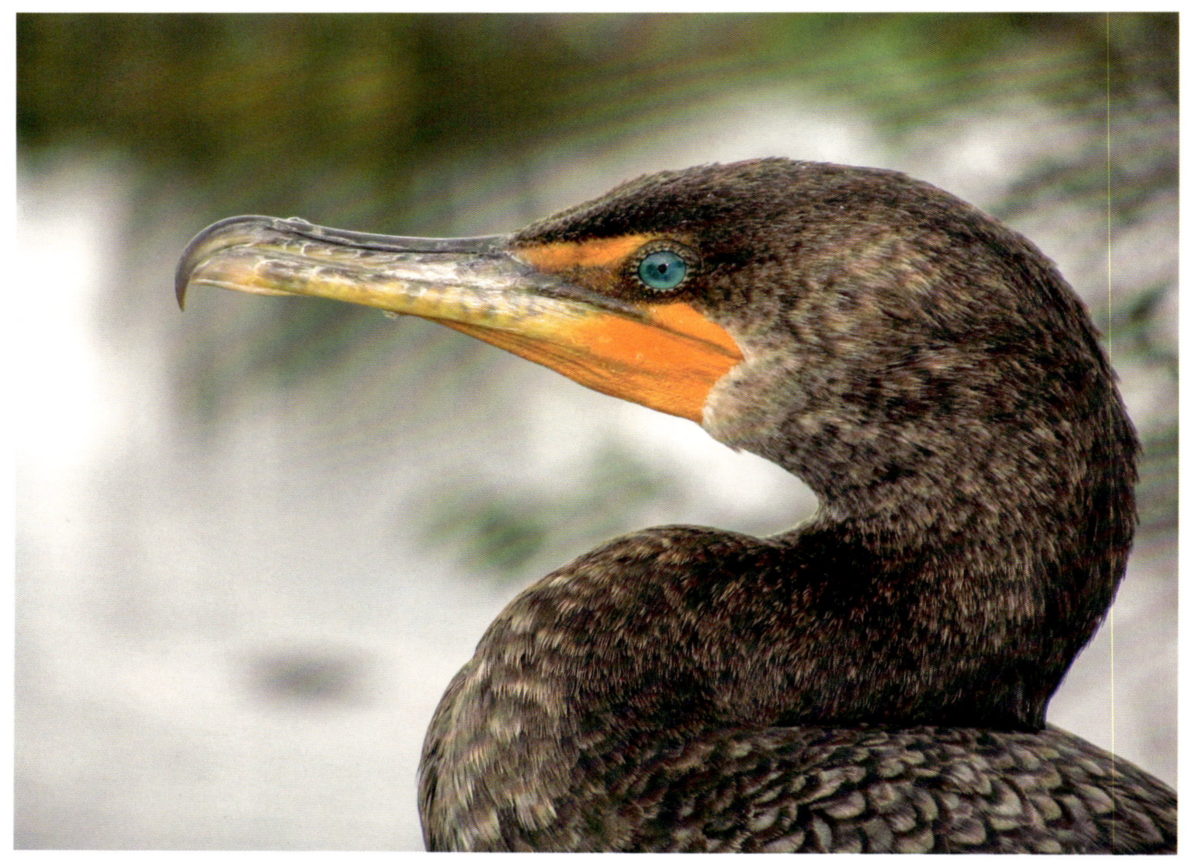

 Double-crested cormorant. *Photo by Howard Hunt.*

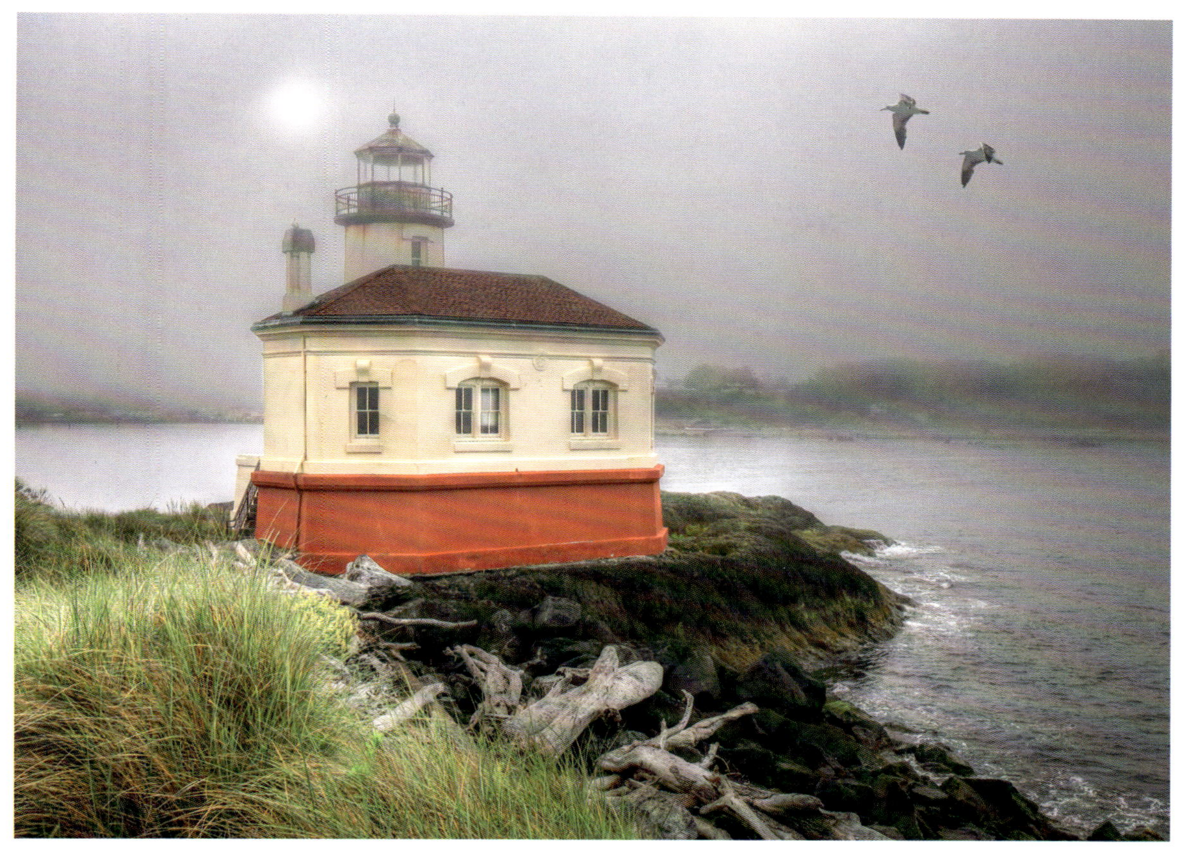

Coquille River Lighthouse, Bandon. The lighthouse, named for the Coquille tribe that resided in the area, was completed in 1896. *Photo by Rudy Dierks.*

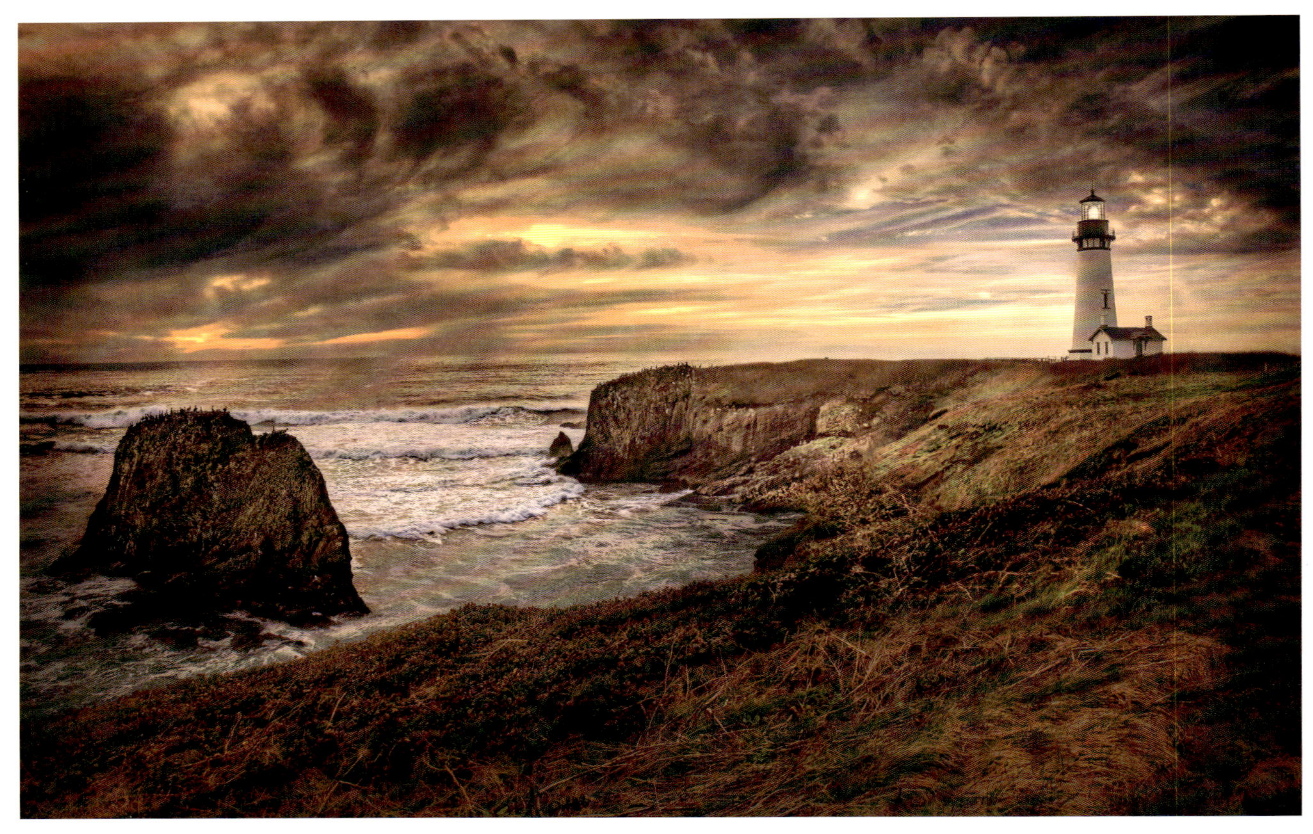

20 Yaquina Head Lighthouse in Newport is the tallest lighthouse in Oregon and stands 93 feet tall. It was first lit in 1873. *Photo by Rudy Dierks.*

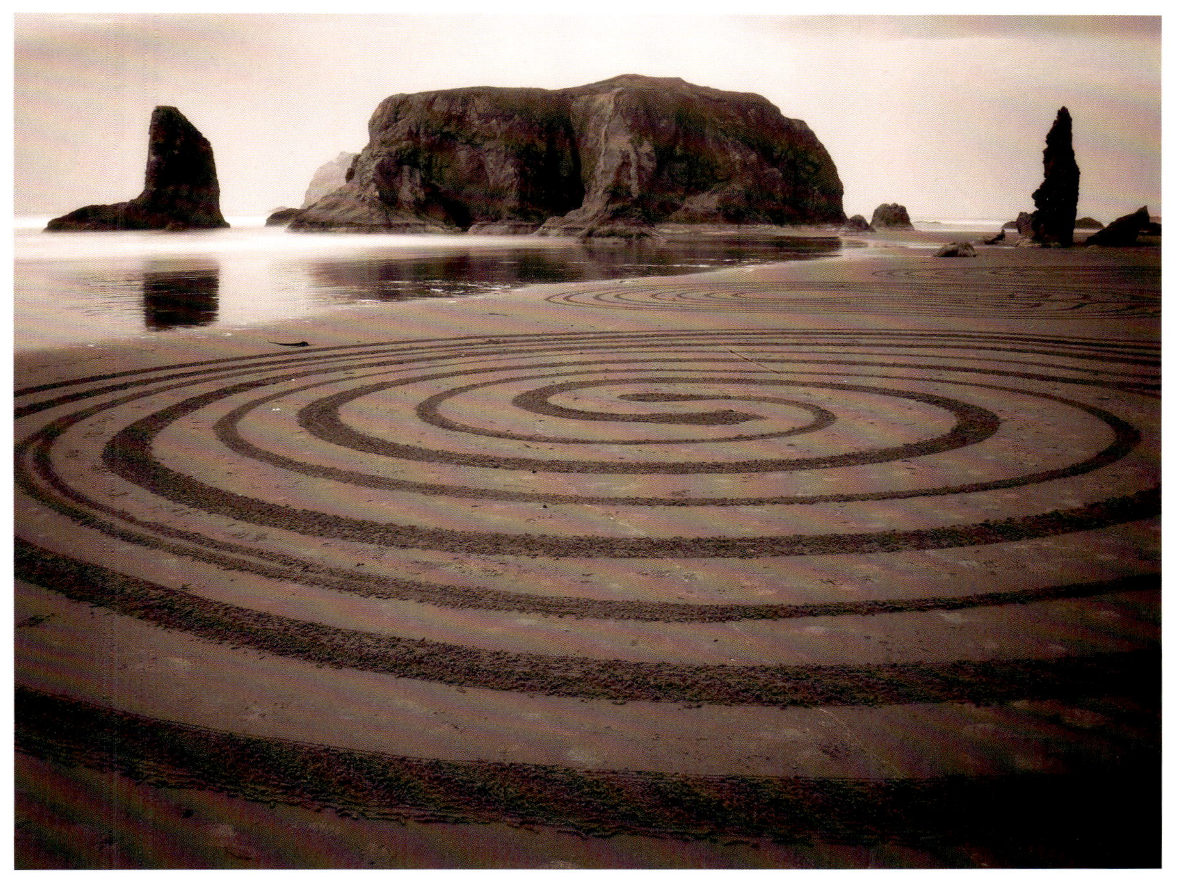

Circles in the sand, Bandon. Labyrinth artwork created by Denny Dyke. *Photo by John Kirk.*   21

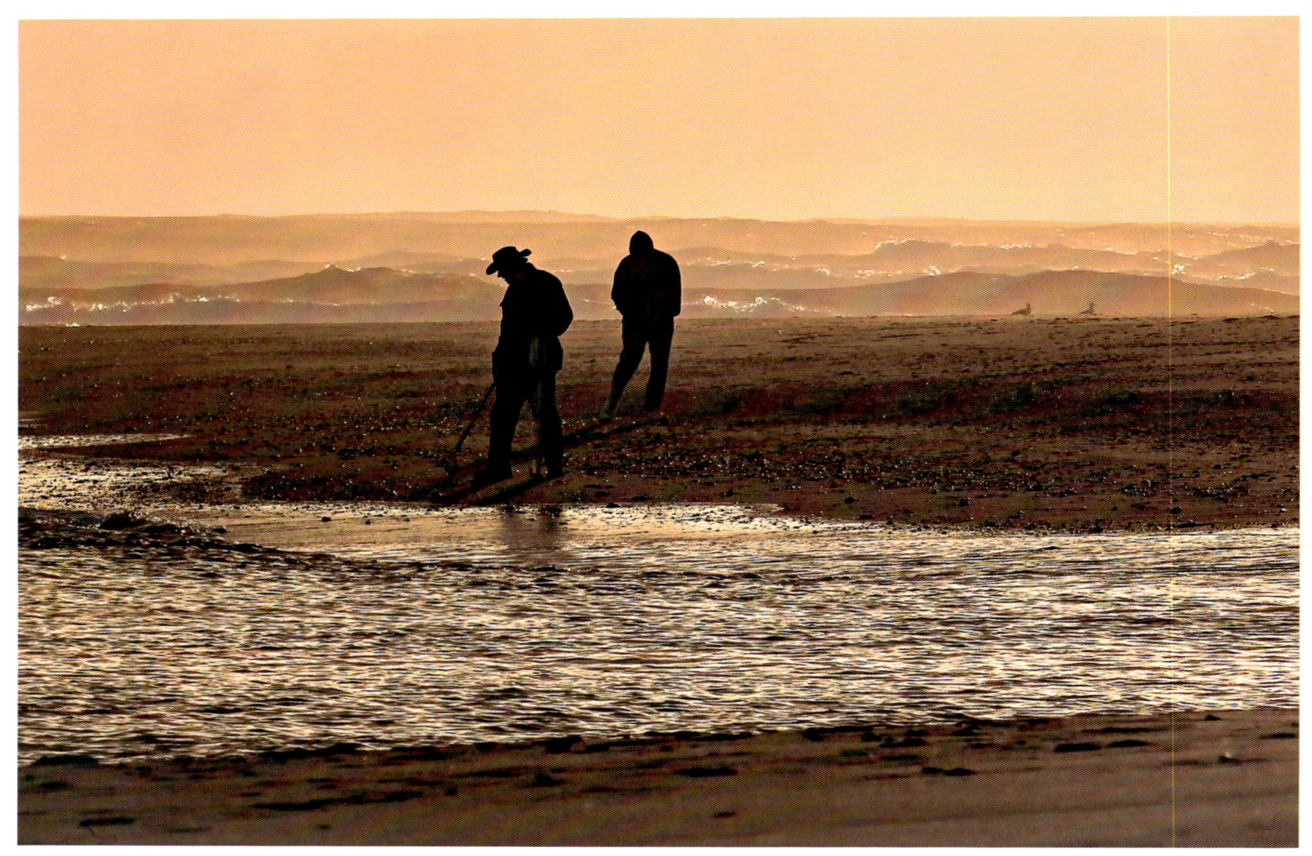

Beachcombing along the Siletz River. The Siletz River flows into the Pacific Ocean near Lincoln City. With ocean waves in the background, beachcombers hunt for agates. *Photo by Terry Fisher.*

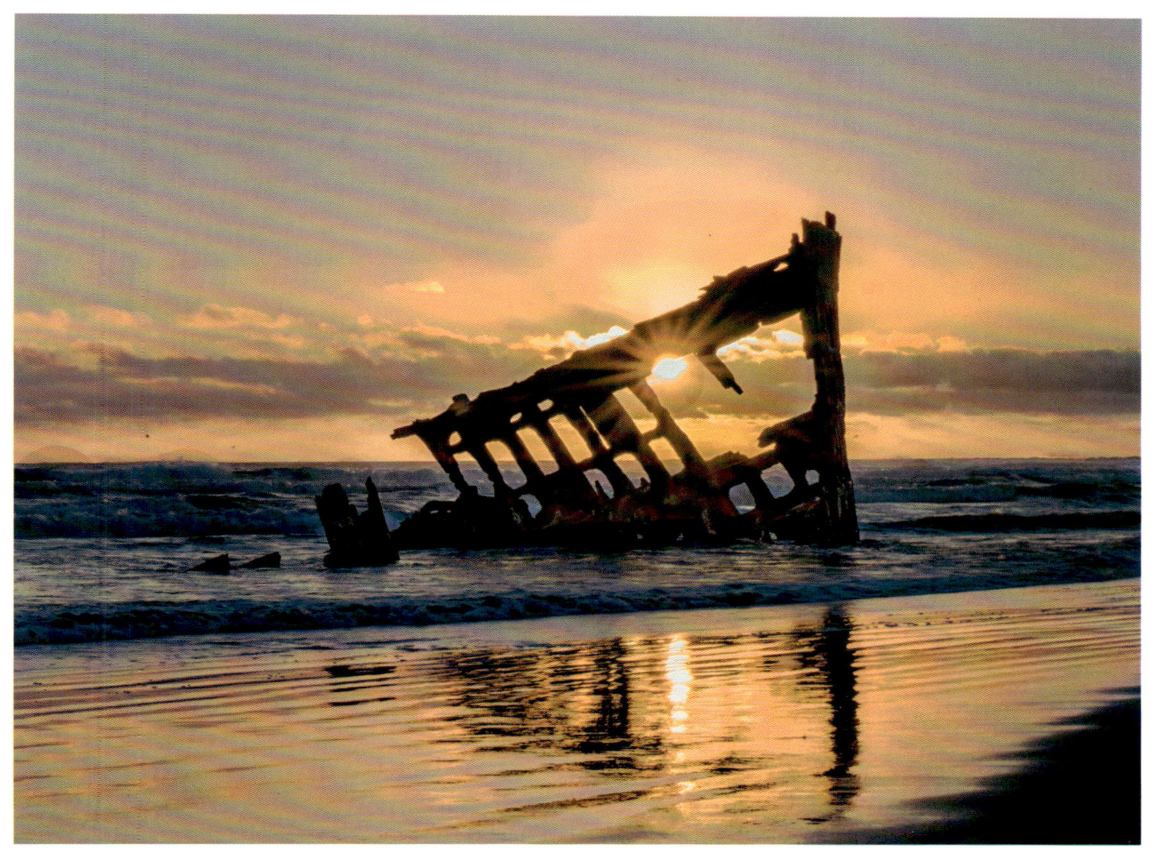

Peter Iredale wreck, Astoria. The sailing ship ran ashore in 1906. Captain H. Lawrence's final toast to his ship was "May God bless you, and may your bones bleach in the sands." *Photo by Doug Farrell.*

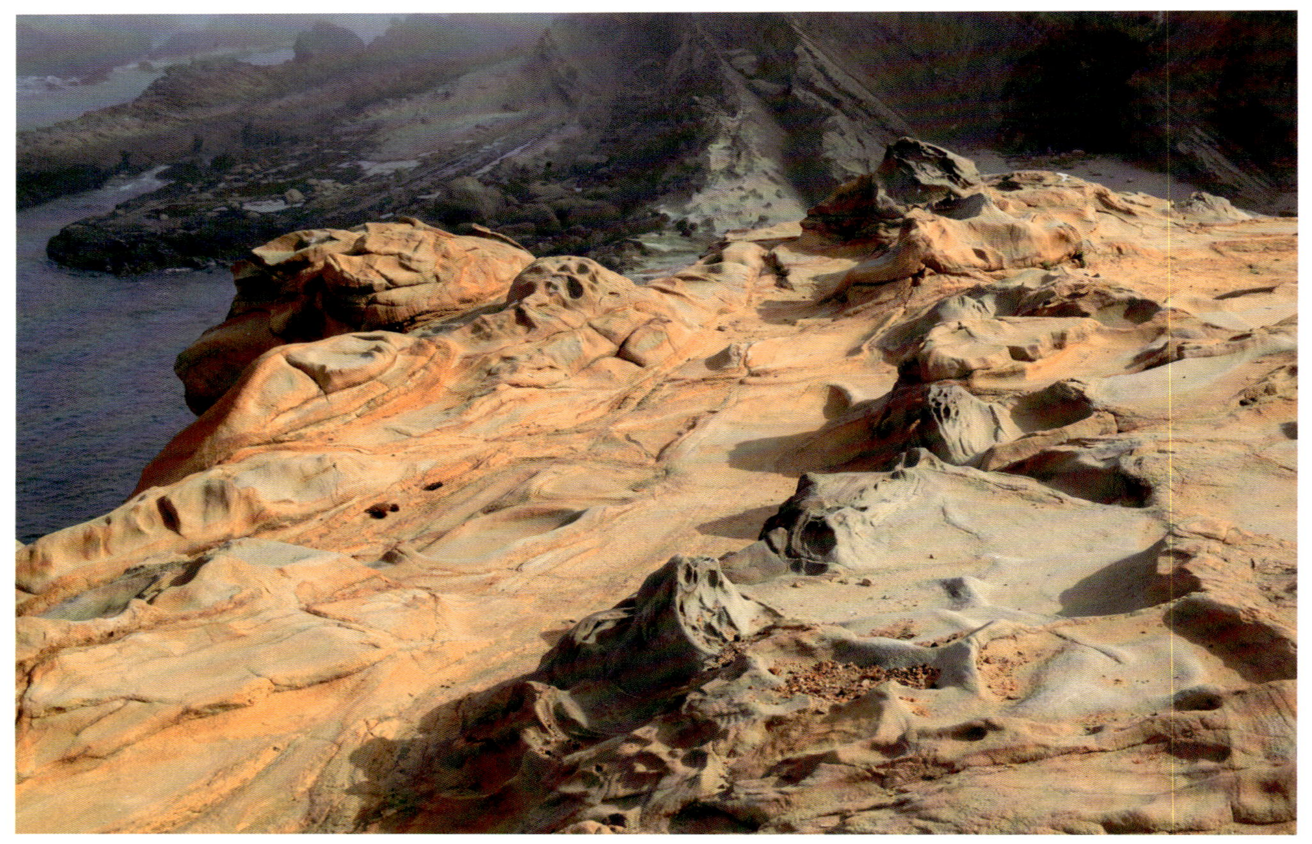

    Shore Acres sandstone formations. *Photo by Neal R. Thompson.*

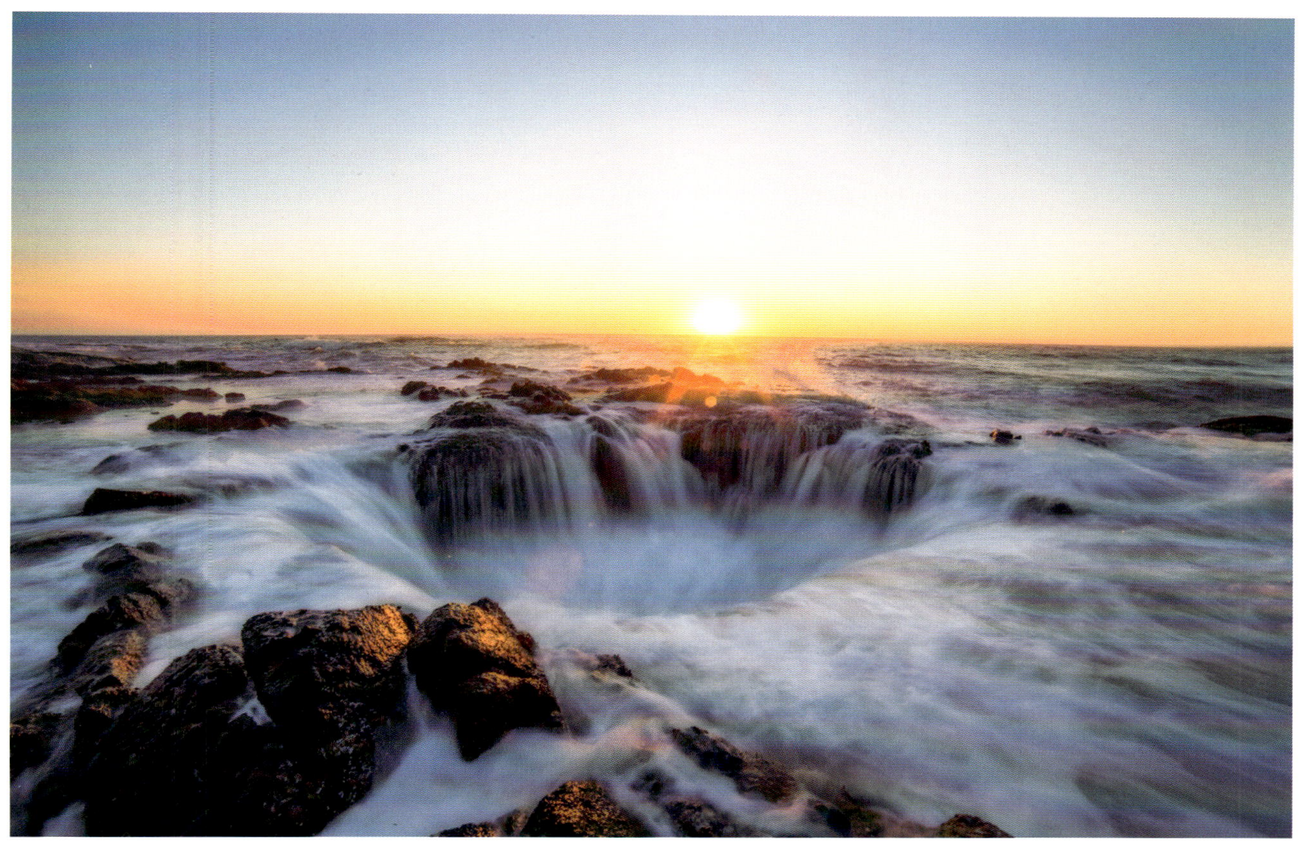

Thor's Well, about three miles south of Yachats, appears to be a magical bottomless sinkhole in the ocean at high tide. However, it is actually a hole in the basalt rock, about 20 feet deep. *Photo by Earshel Hogan.*

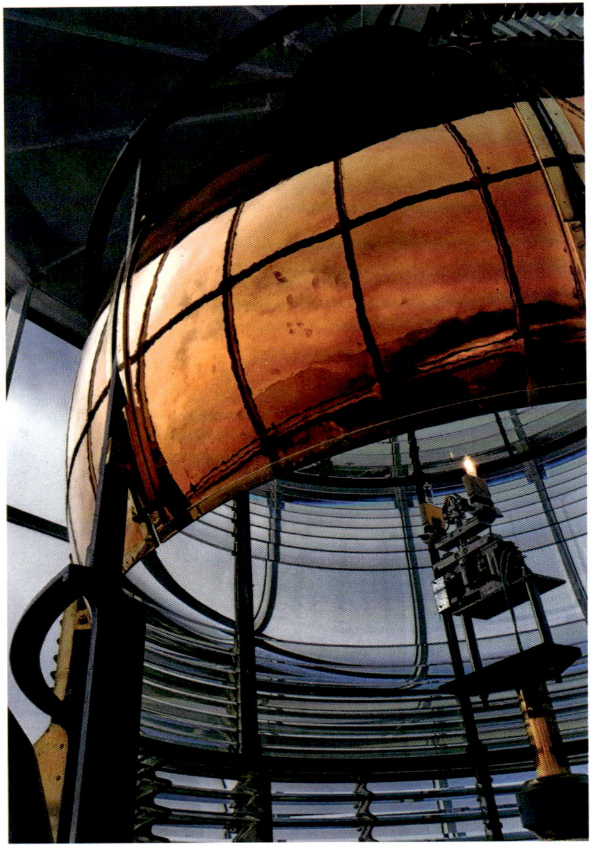

Fresnel lens, manufactured in Paris in 1868, Yaquina Head Lighthouse. *Photo by Richard Krieger.*

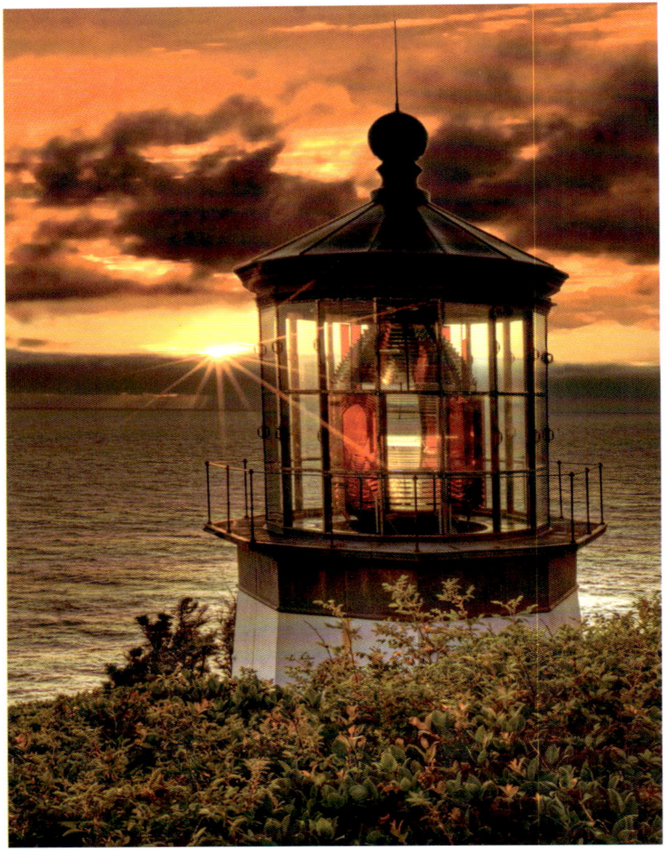

Cape Meares Lighthouse. Located ten miles west of Tillamook on Cape Meares, this lighthouse was built in 1890. *Photo by Rudy Dierks.*

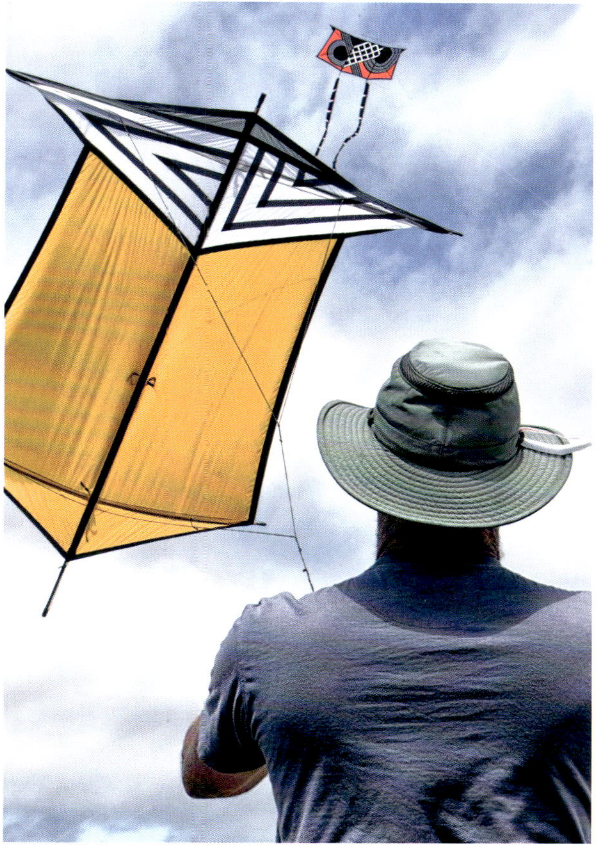

Southern Oregon Kite Festival in Brookings. *Photo by Richard Krieger.*

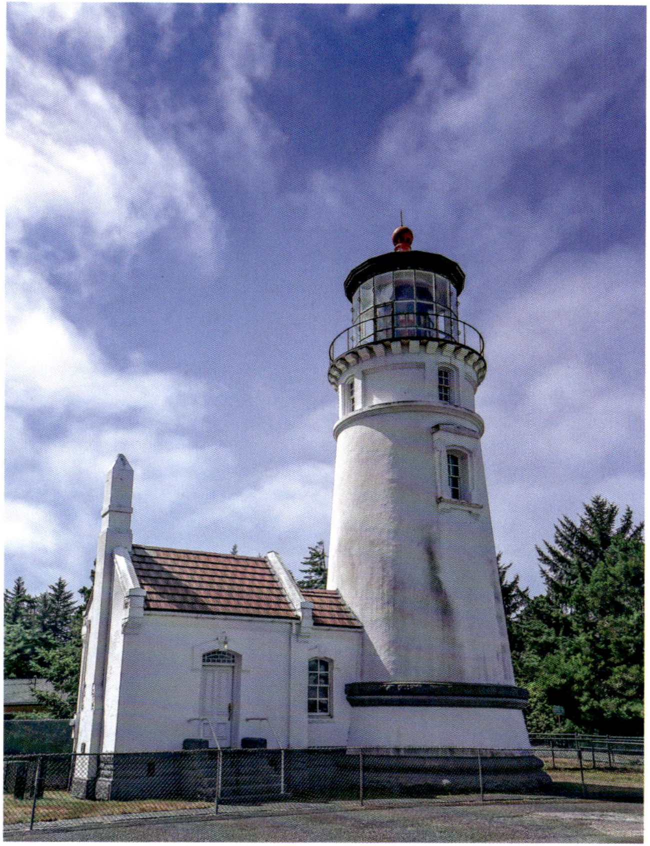

Umpqua River Lighthouse at Winchester Bay, built in 1855. *Photo by Terry Fisher.*

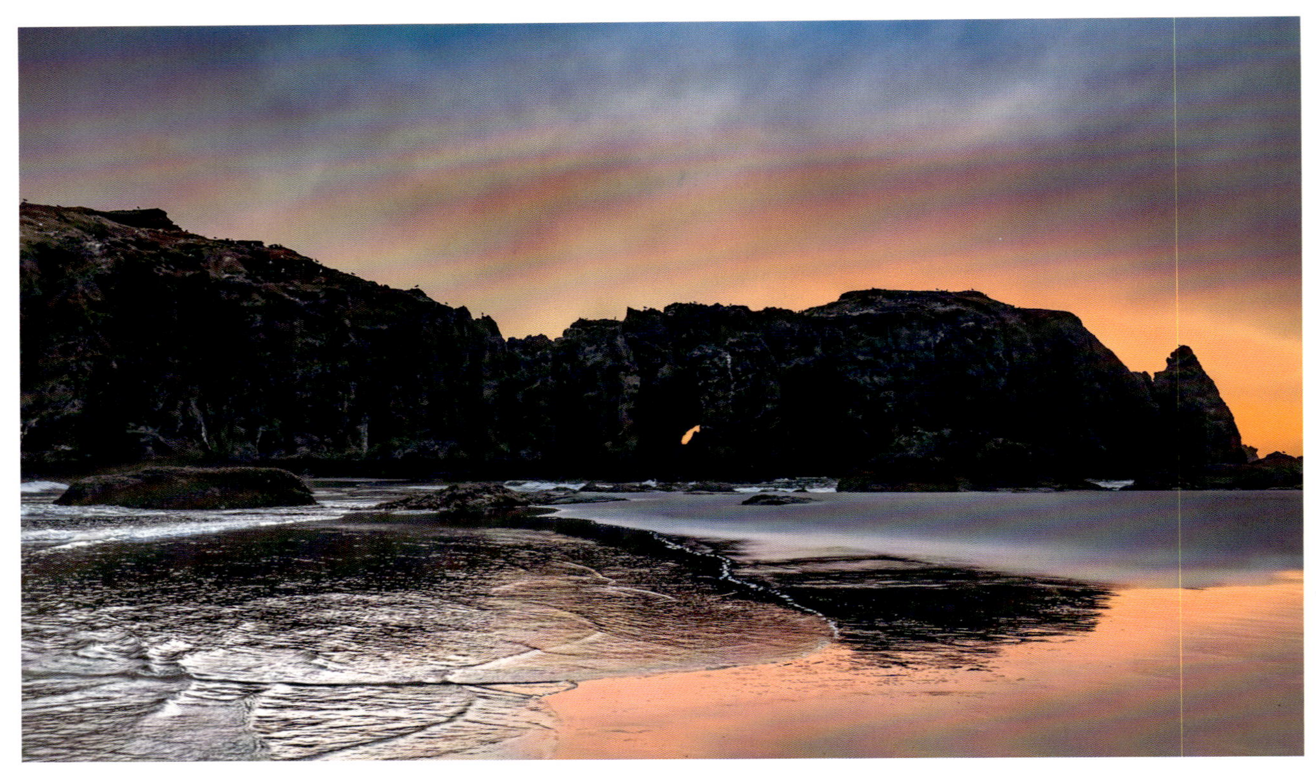

 Bandon Beach sunset. *Photo by Sue Stendebach.*

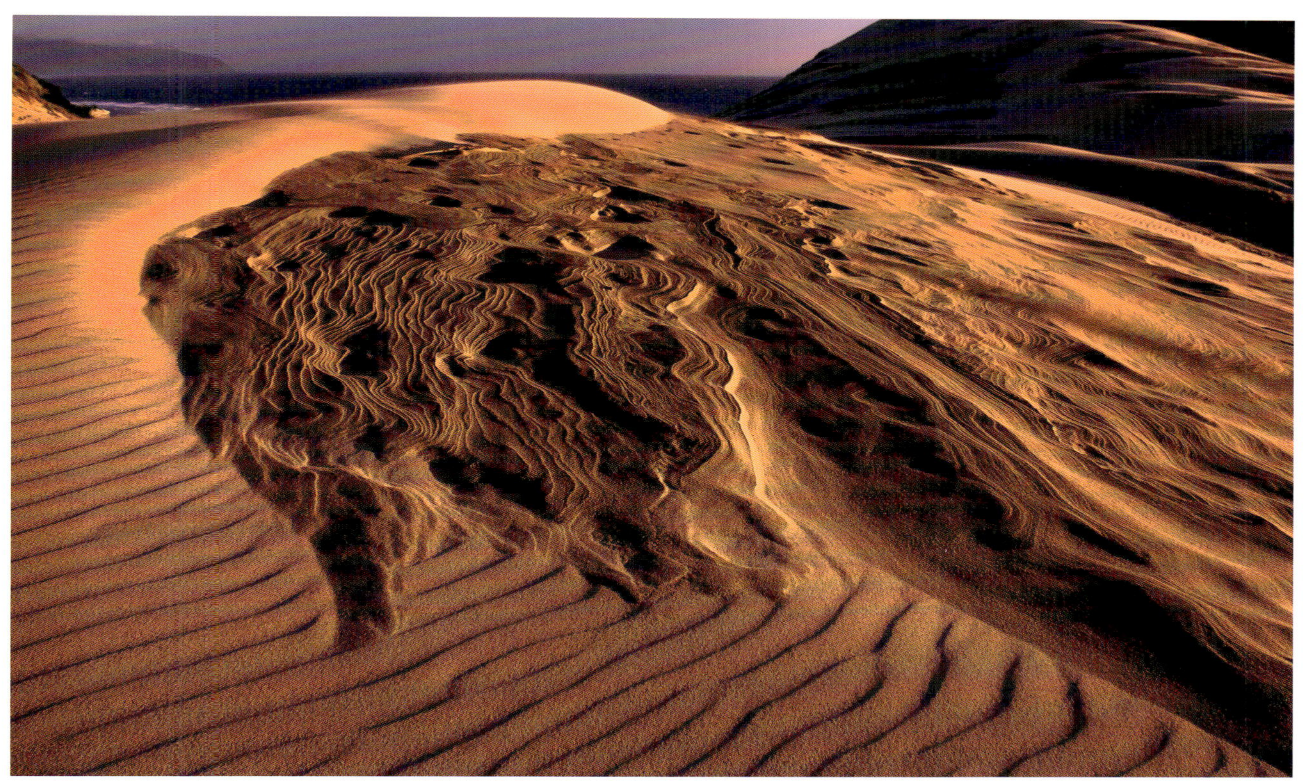

Sand dune at Pacific City. *Photo by Clem Paslack.* 29

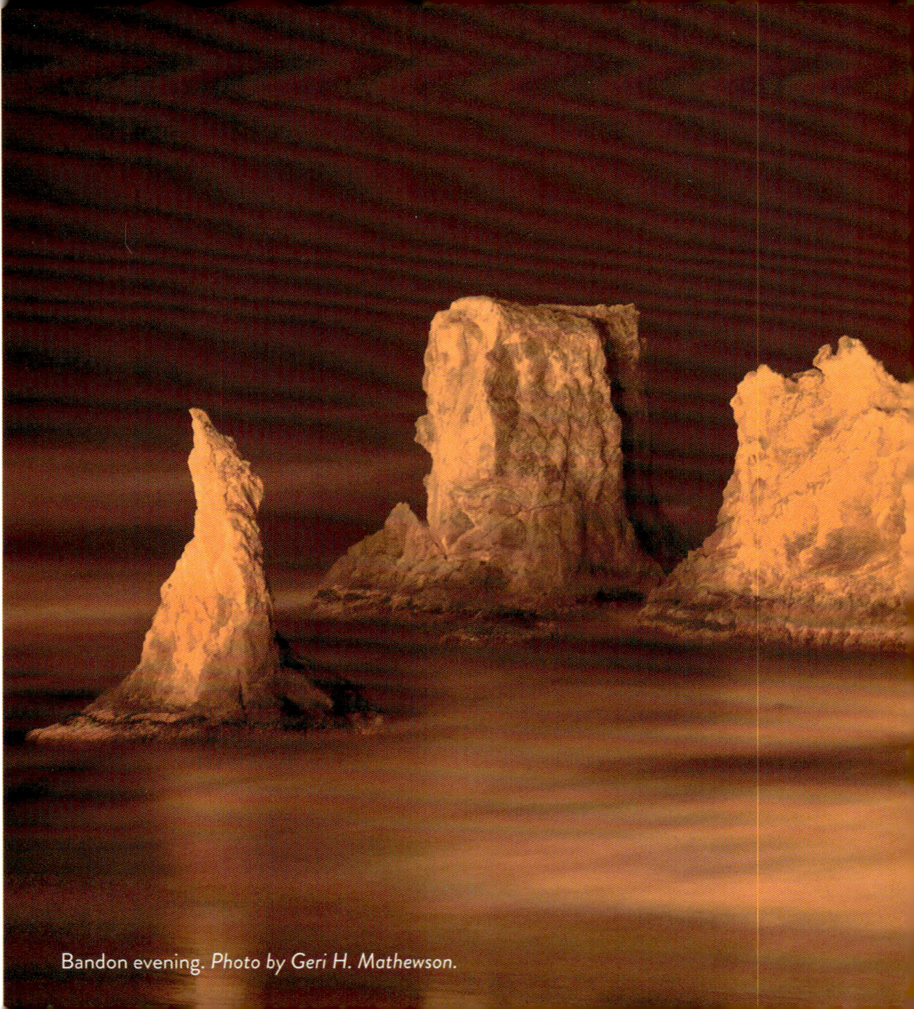

Bandon evening. *Photo by Geri H. Mathewson.*

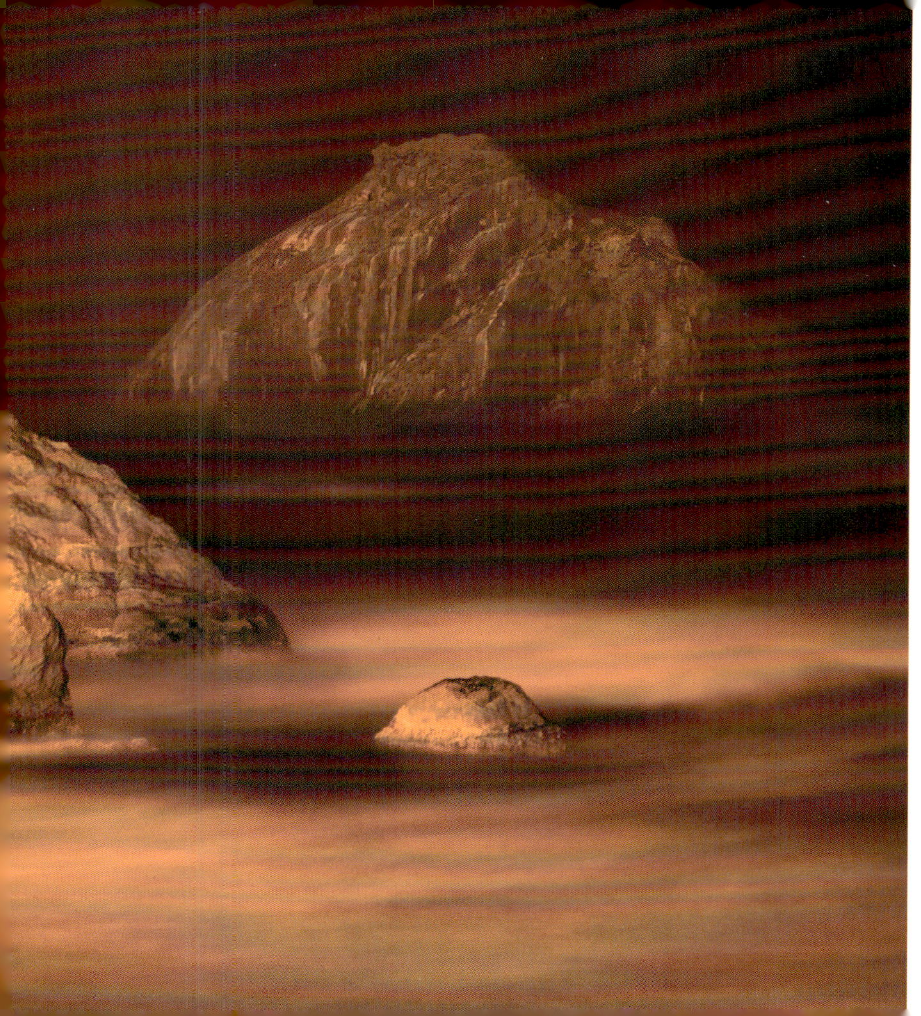

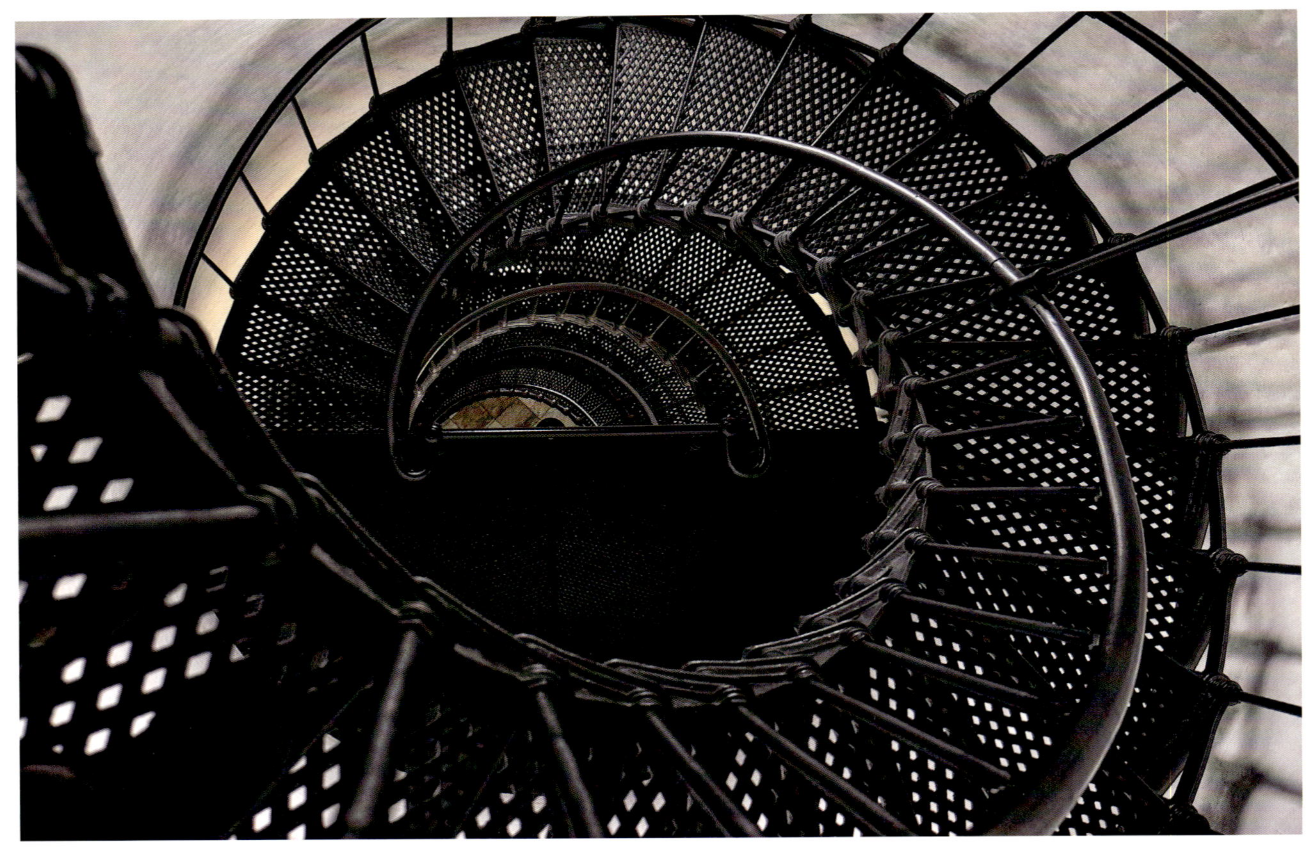

  Yaquina Head Lighthouse's 114-step spiral staircase. *Photo by Richard Krieger.*

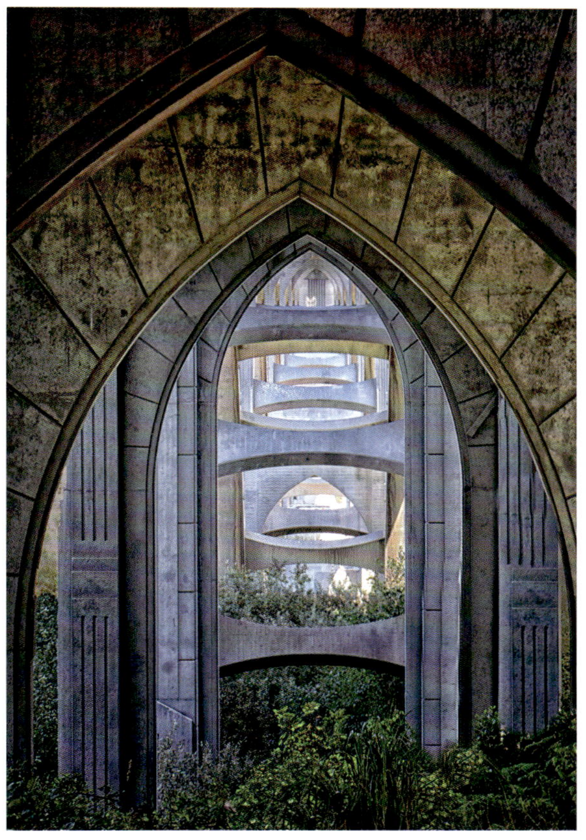

Arches under McCullough Memorial Bridge, North Bend. The bridge spans Coos Bay and was built in 1936. *Photo by Barbara Tricarico.*

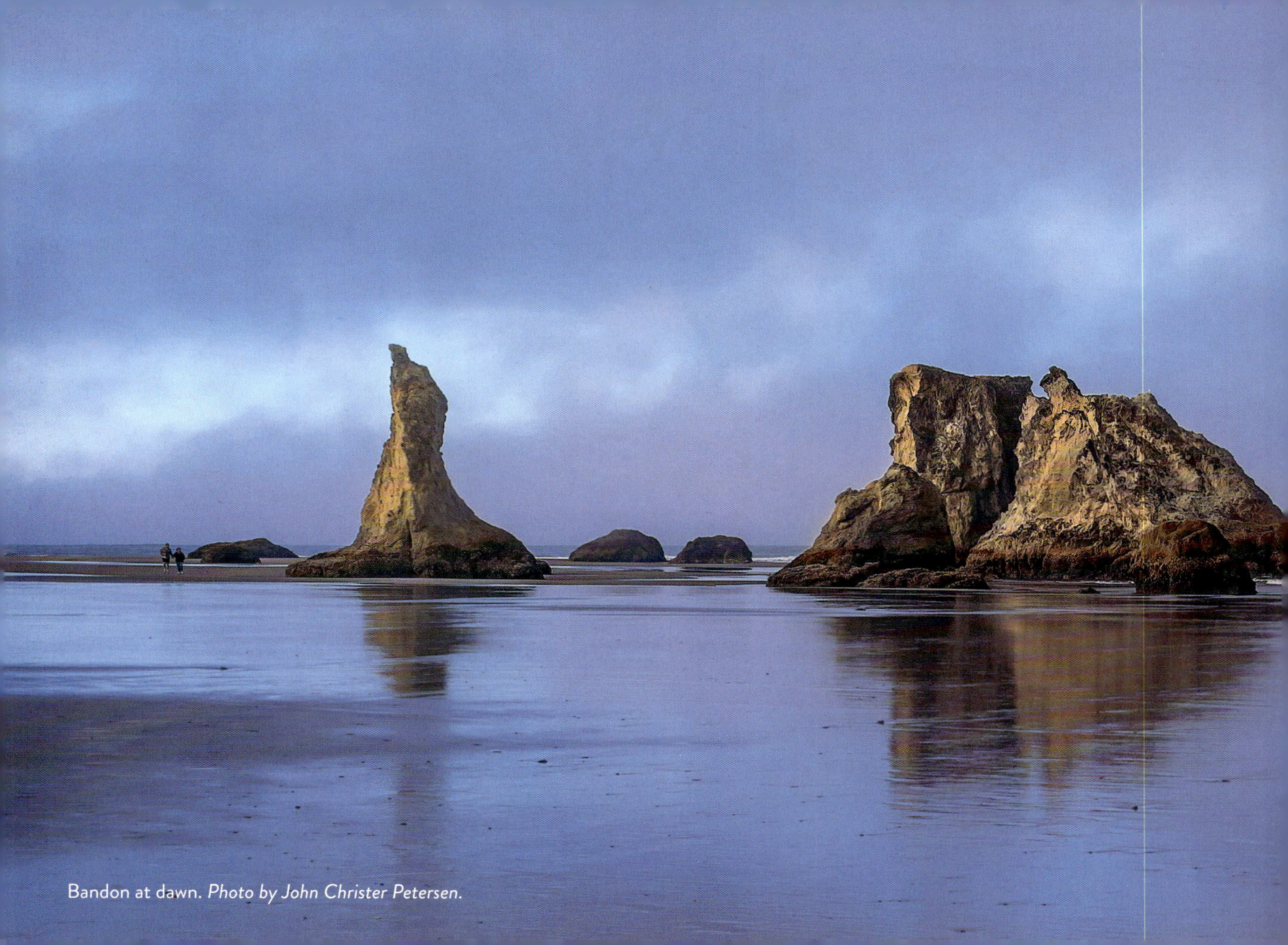

Bandon at dawn. *Photo by John Christer Petersen.*

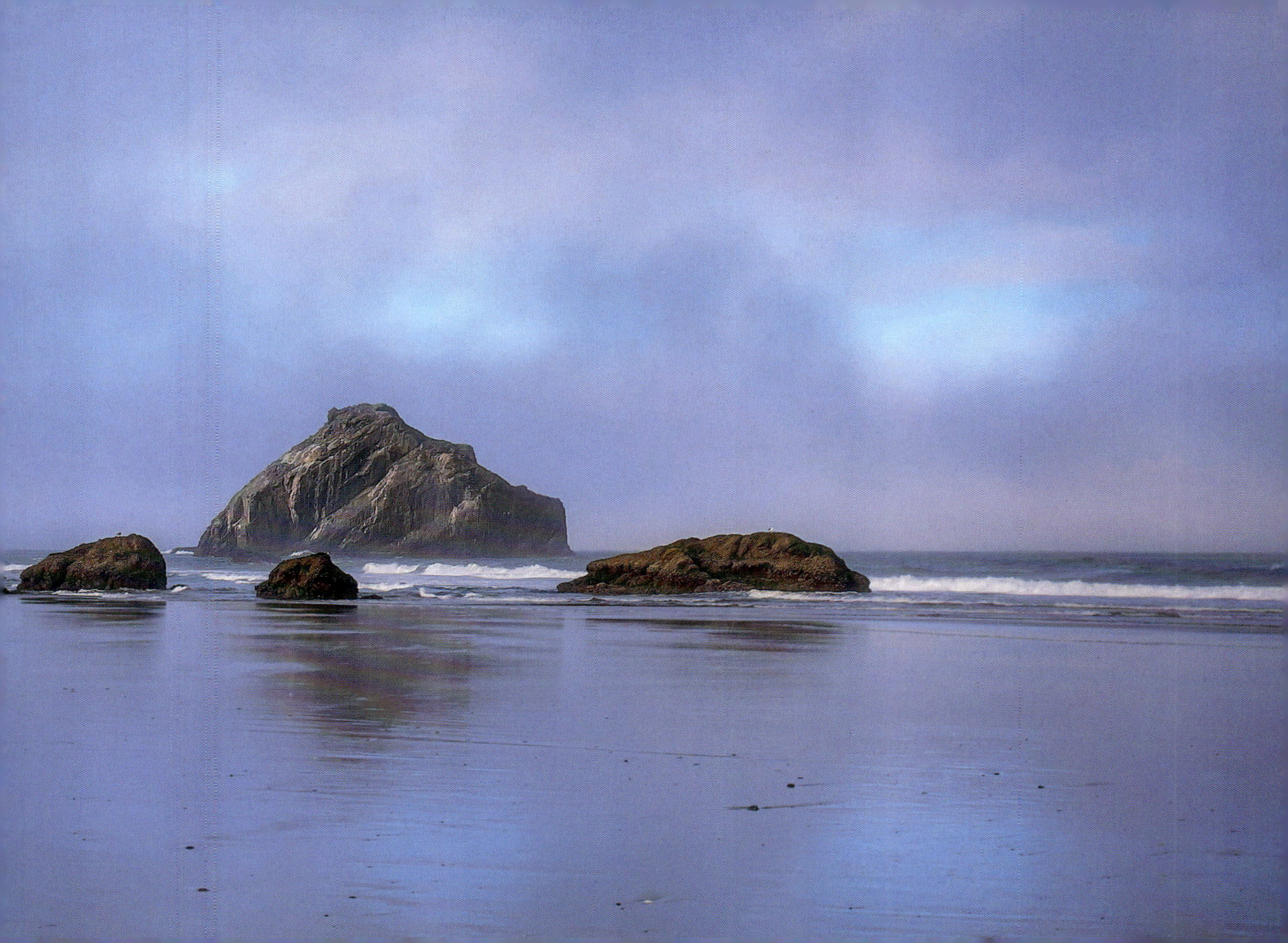

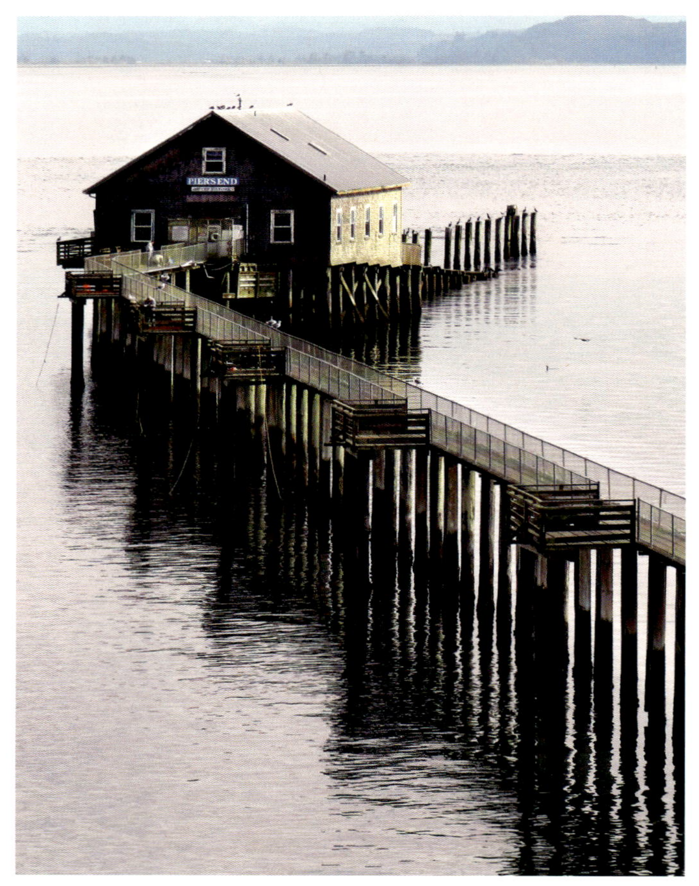

 Pier's End Boathouse in Garibaldi, originally a lifeboat station, built in 1936. *Photo by Charles Hillestad.*

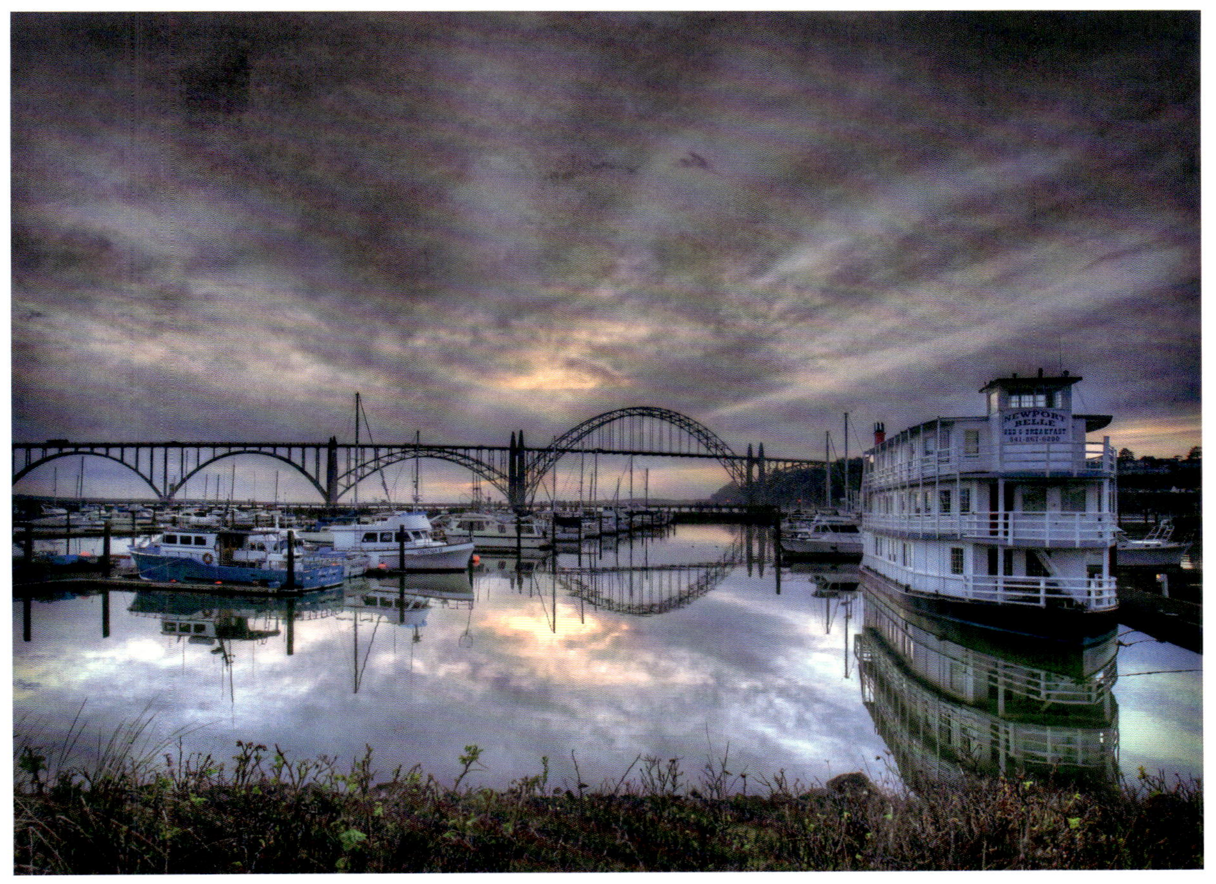

Yaquina Bay Bridge, built in 1936, and *Newport Belle* riverboat. *Photo by Rudy Dierks.*   37

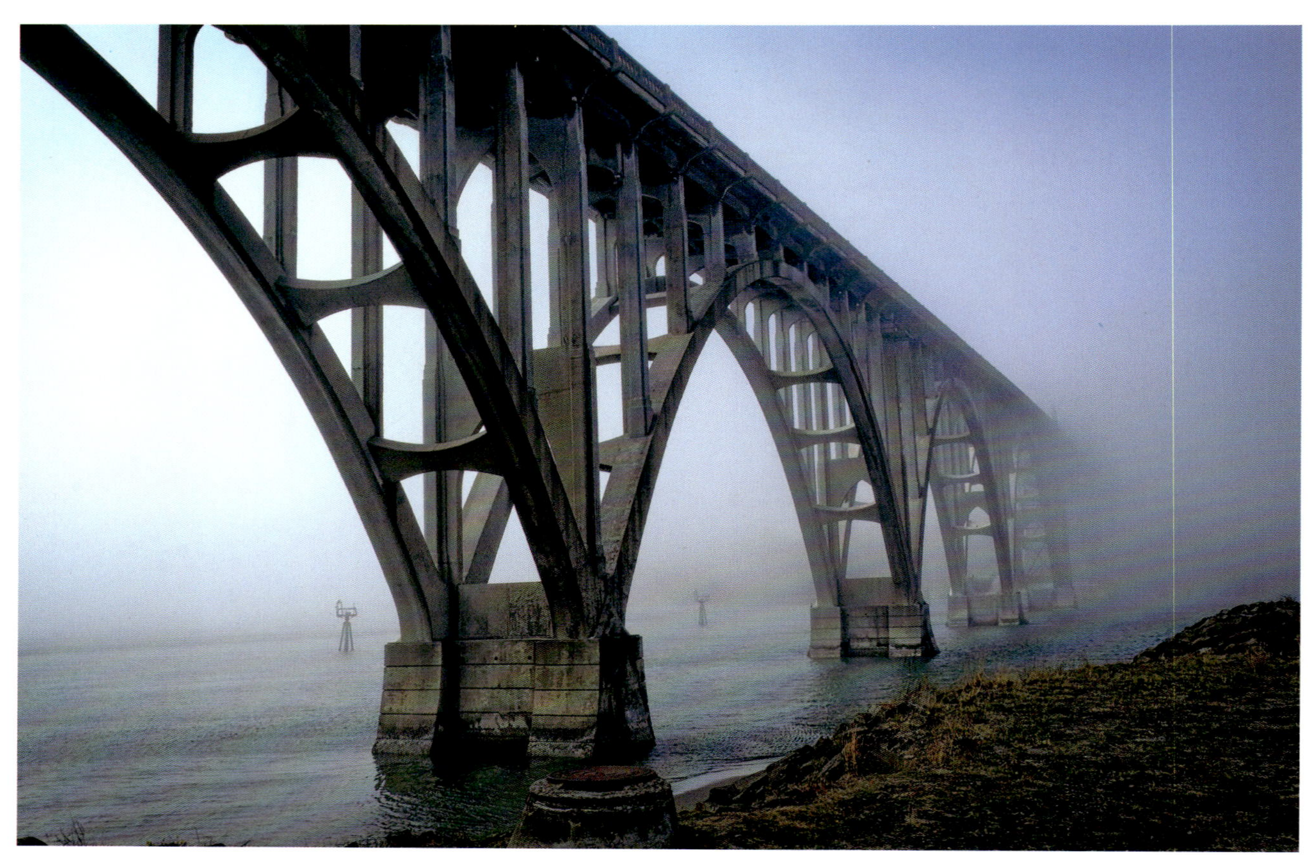

38   Yaquina Bay Bridge, Newport. *Photo by Richard Krieger.*

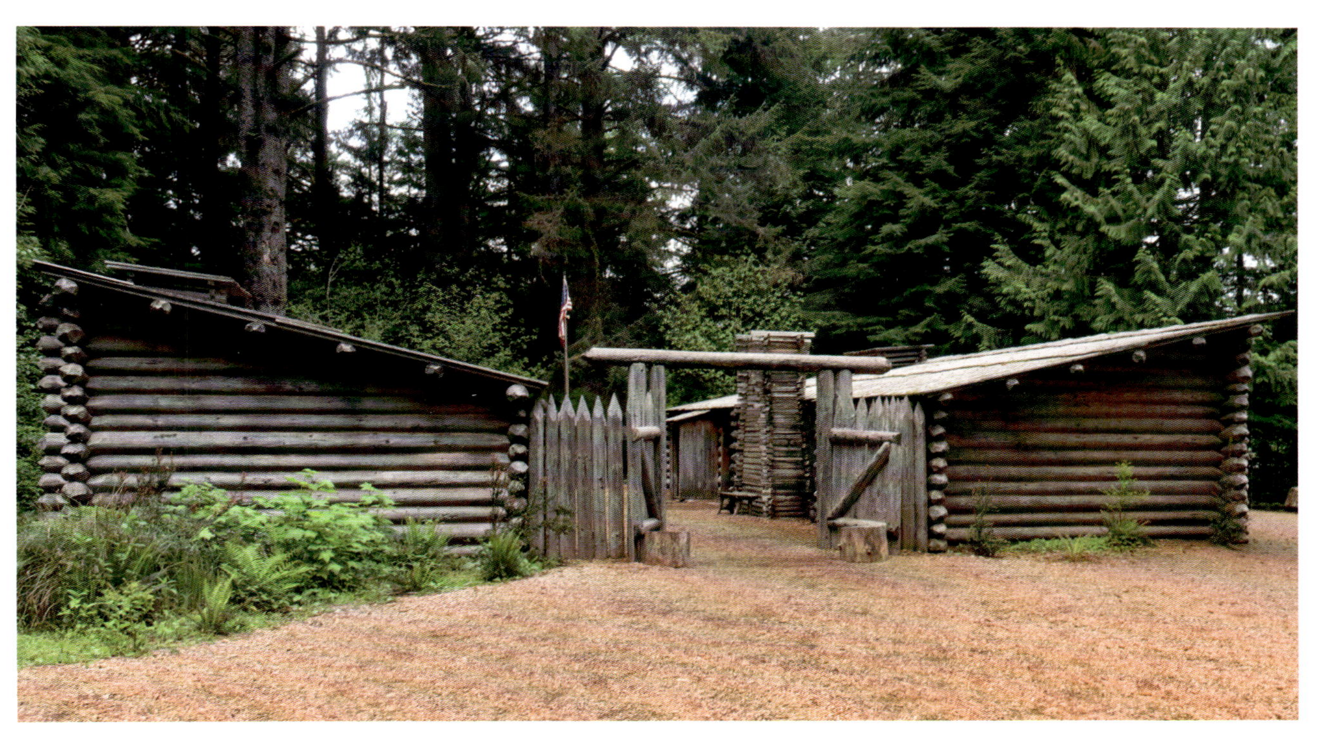

Fort Clatsop, near Astoria. From December 1805 to March 1806, Fort Clatsop was the winter encampment for Lewis and Clark's Corps of Discovery. *Photo by Barbara Tricarico.*

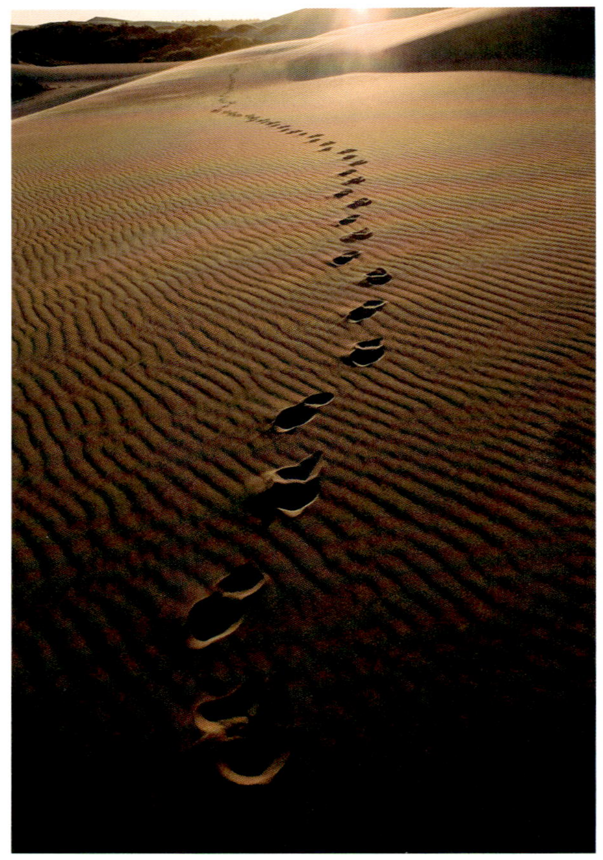

40   Oregon Dunes. *Photo by David Lorenz Winston.*

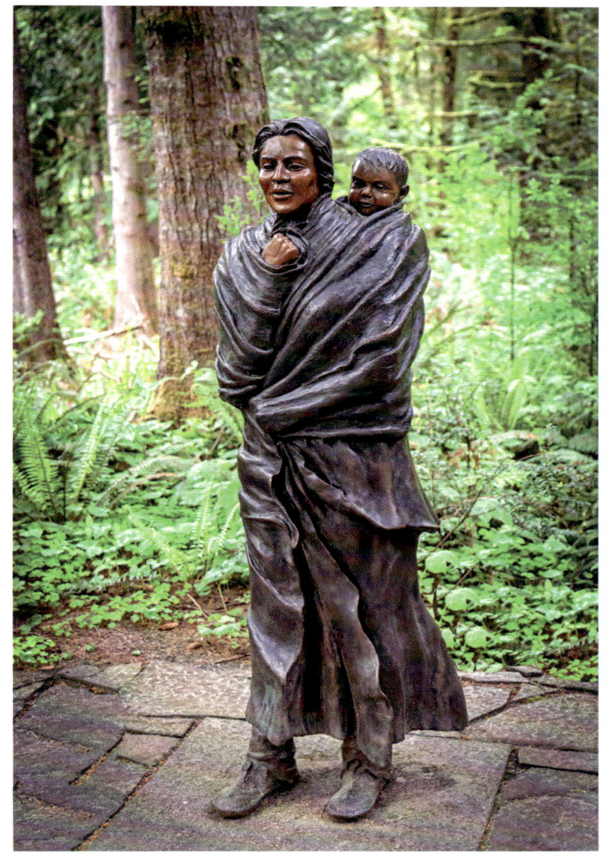

Sacagawea with Her Baby, Jean Baptiste Charbonneau, at Fort Clatsop by artist Jim Demetro. *Photo by Barbara Tricarico.*   41

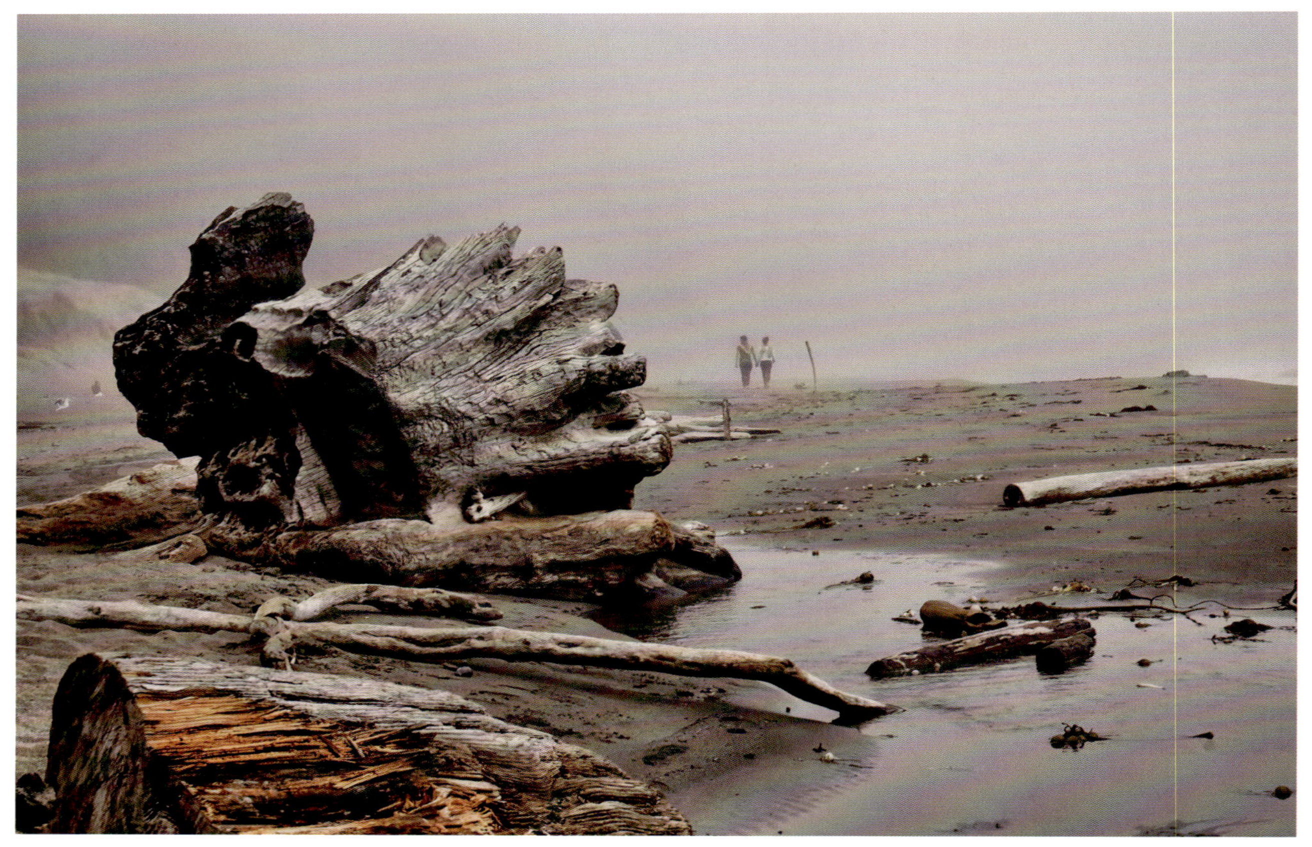

   Battle Rock Wayside Park in Port Orford. *Photo by Richard Krieger.*

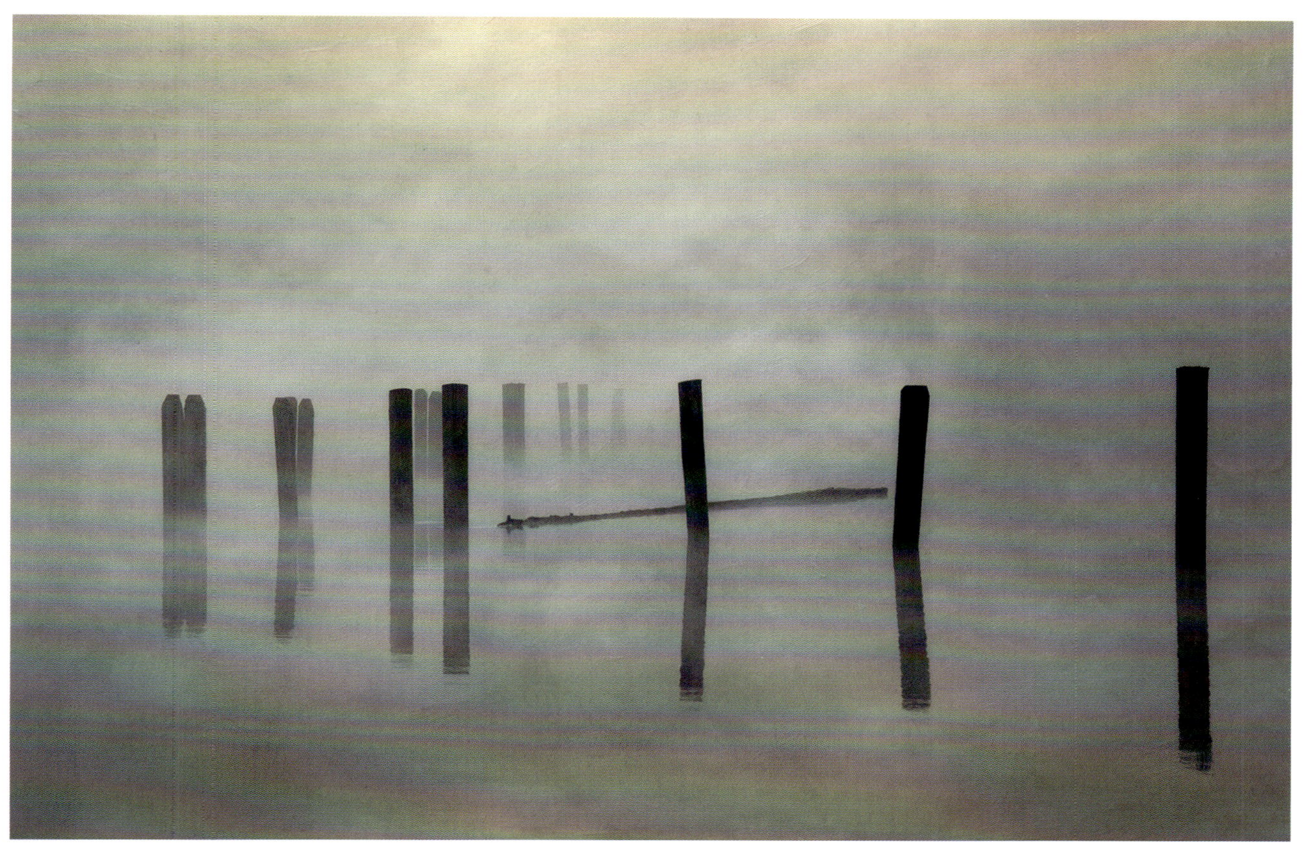

Dawn on Coos Bay. *Photo by David Lorenz Winston.*   43

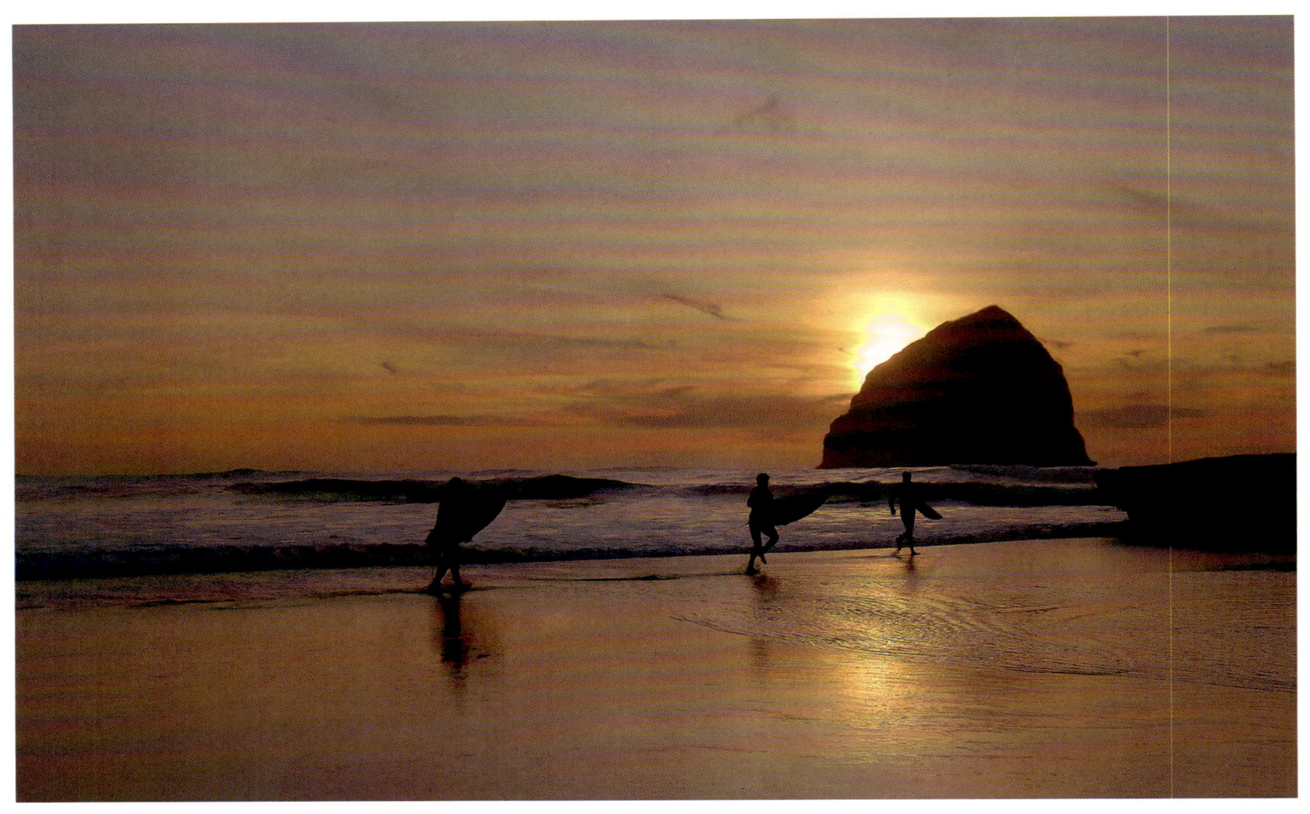

   Surfers at Pacific City. *Photo by Clem Paslack.*

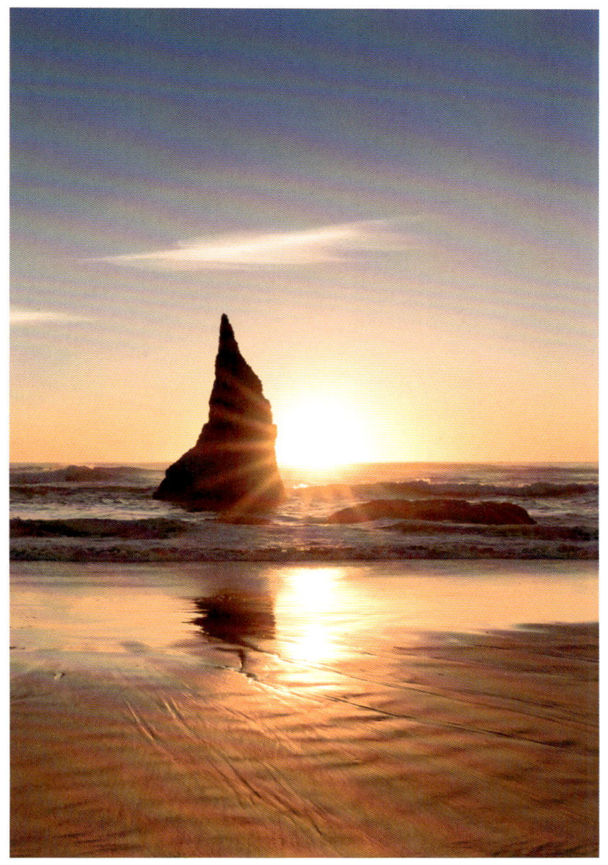

Wizard's Hat rock formation, Bandon Beach. *Photo by Barbara Tricarico.*   45

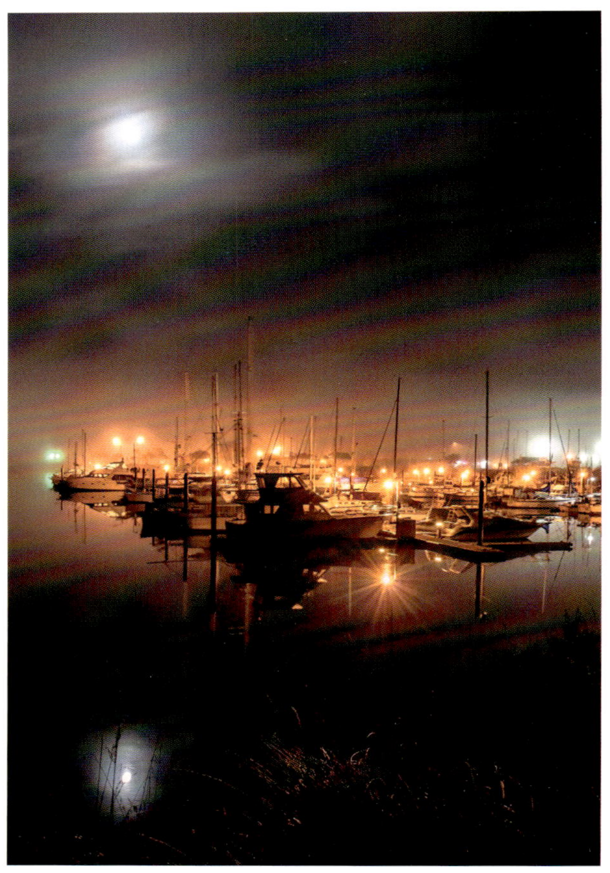

    Charleston Harbor. *Photo by Sue Newman.*

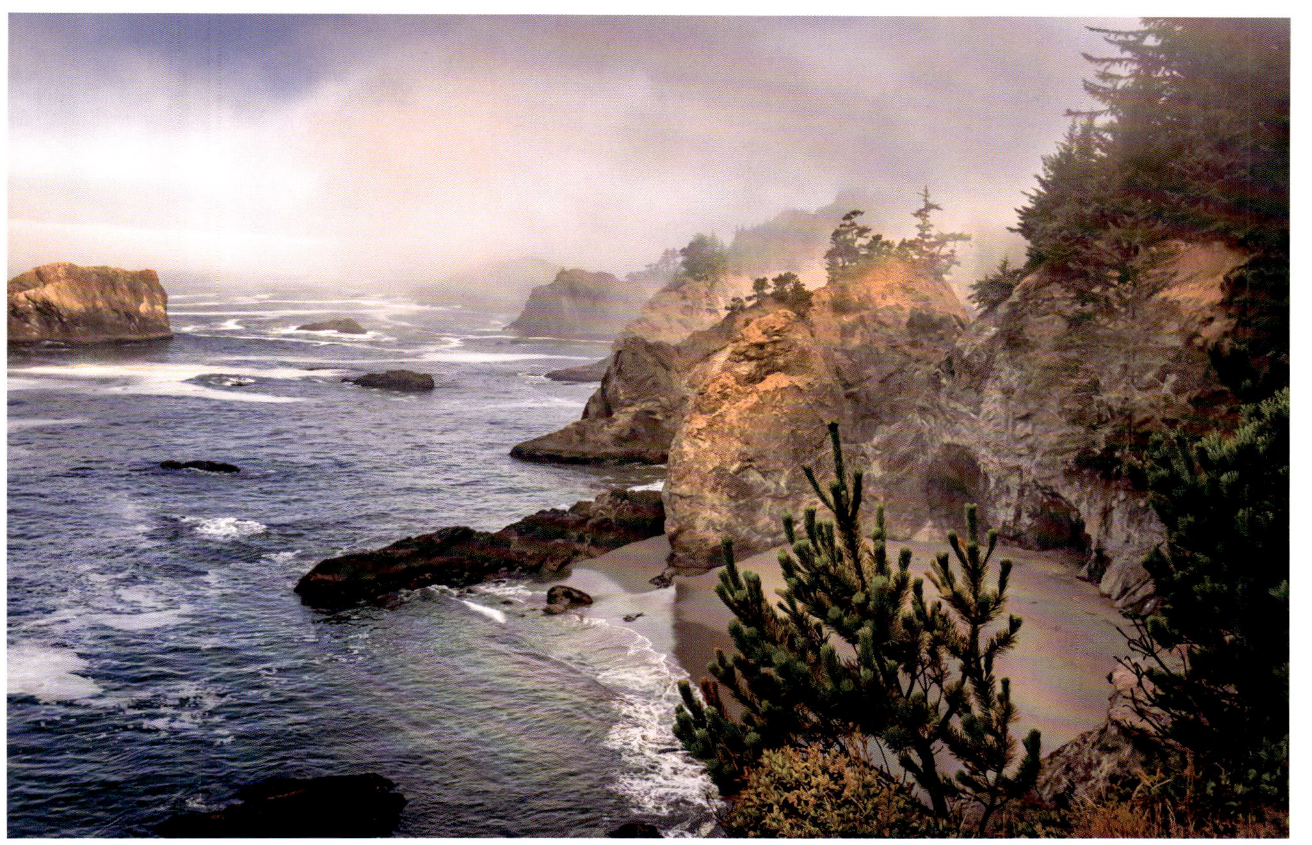

Thunder Rock Cove, Brookings. *Photo by Ellen Ahern.*   47

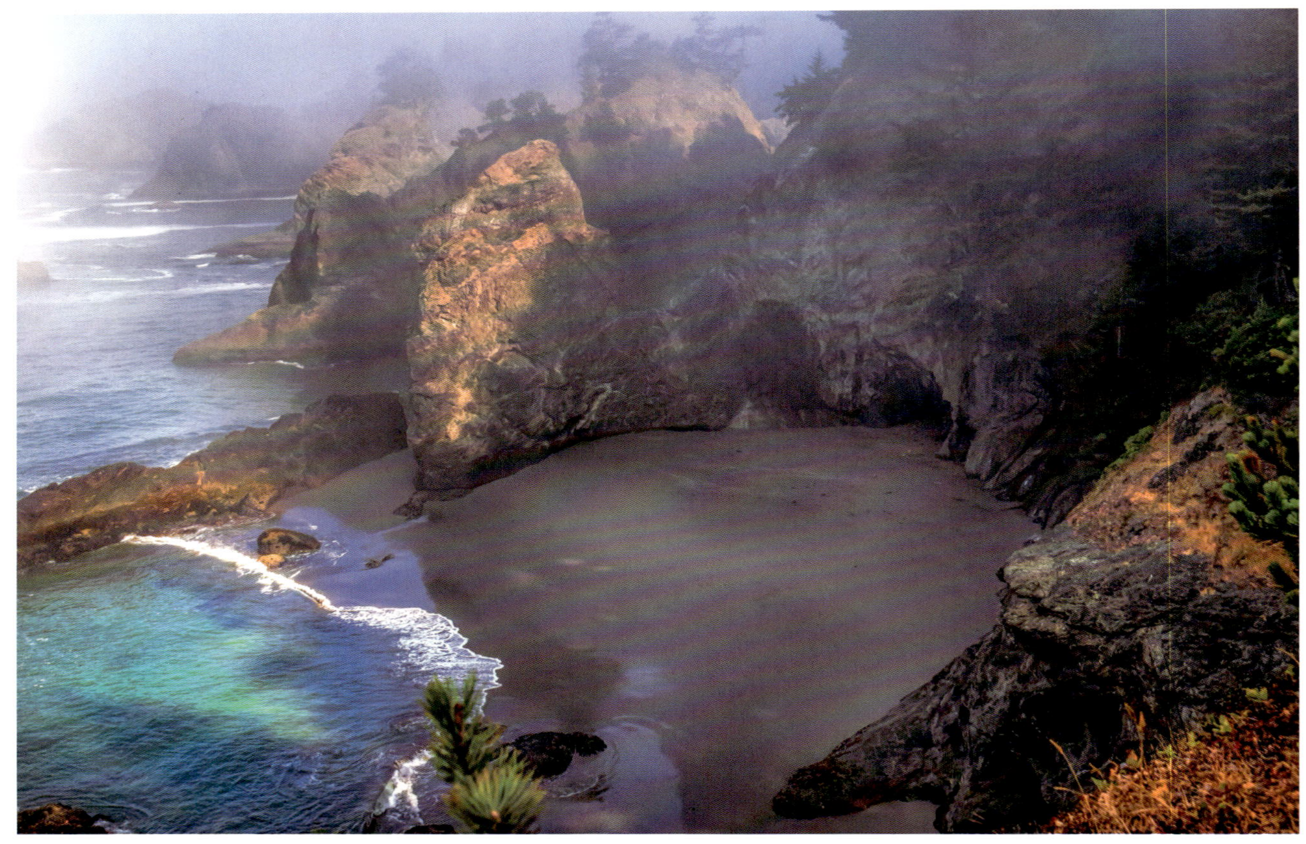

48   Thunder Rock Cove, Brookings. *Photo by Ellen Ahern.*

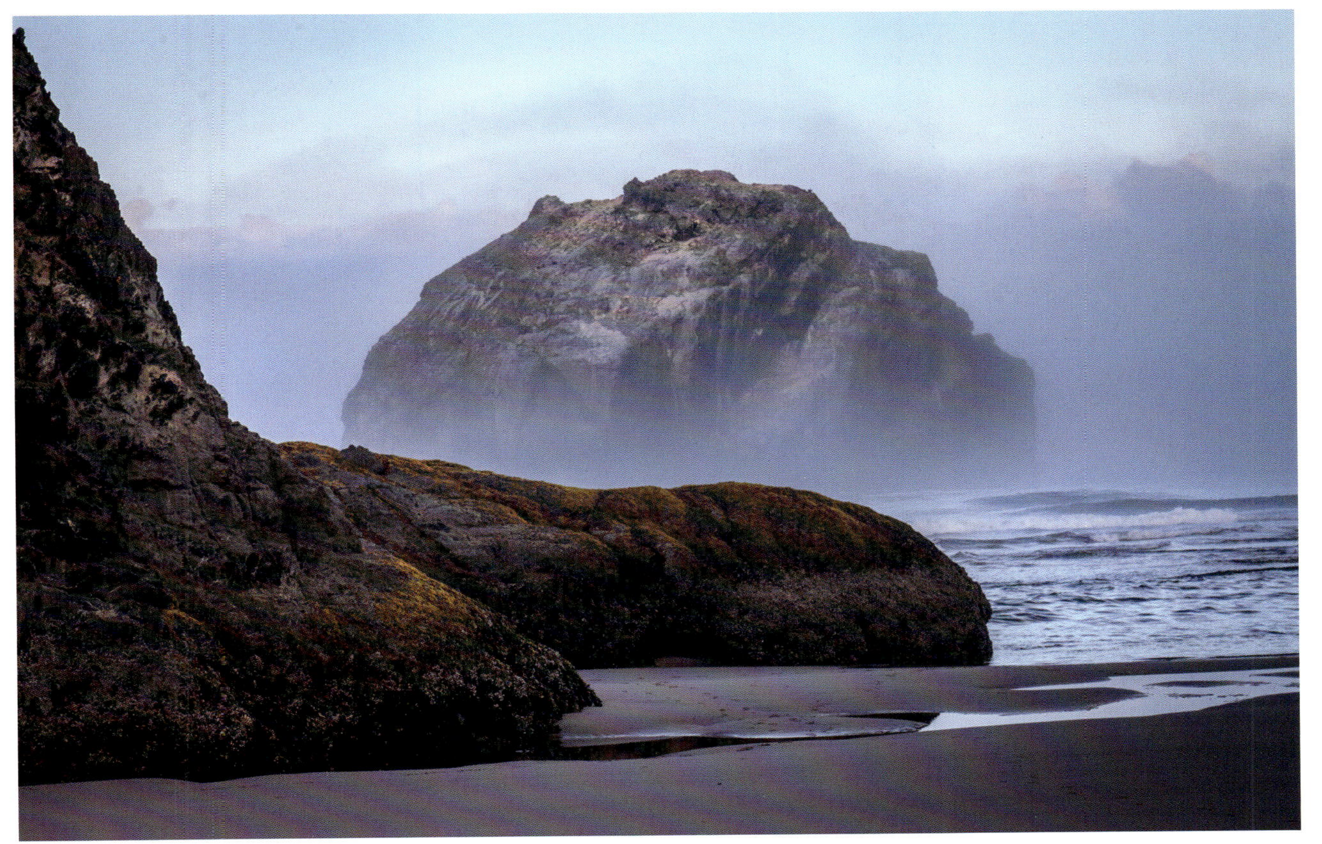

Face Rock, Bandon Beach. *Photo by Ellen Ahern.*   49

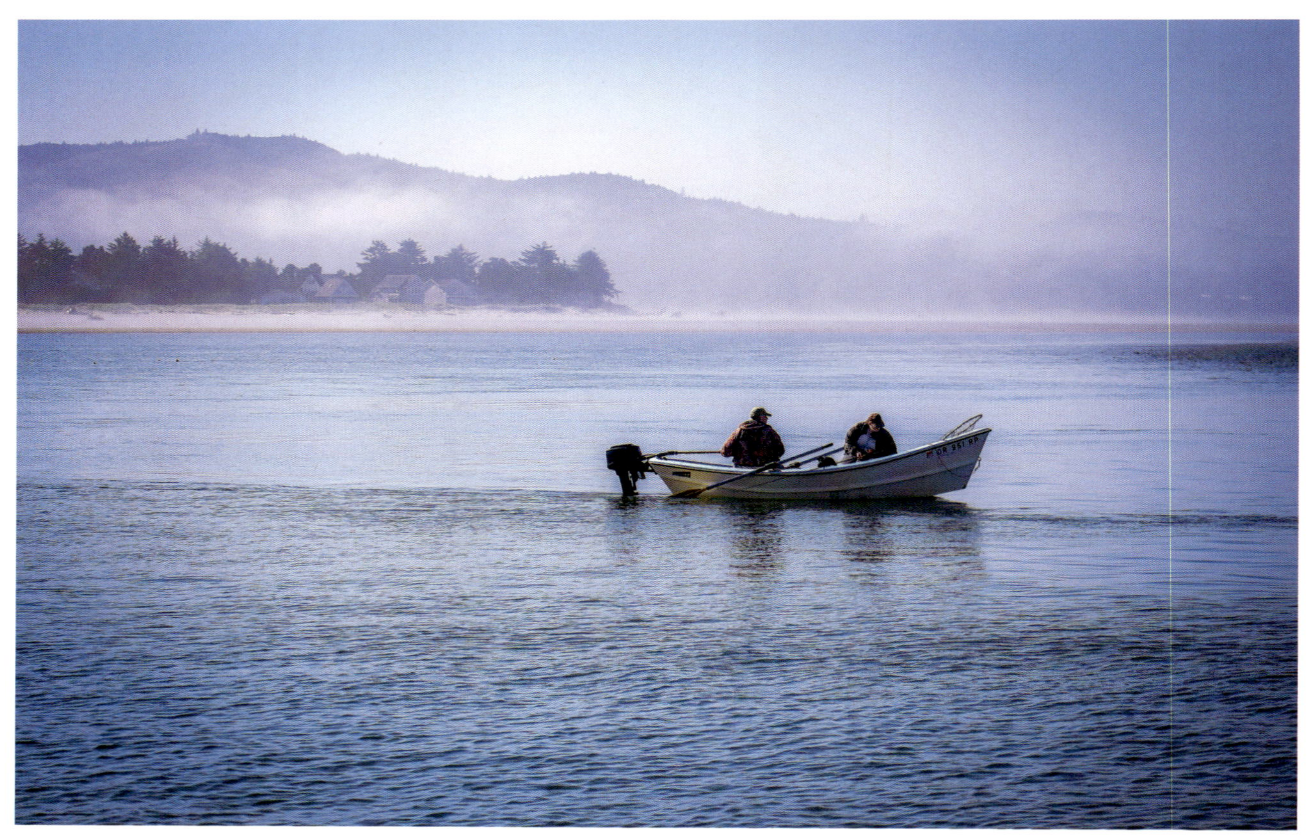

50   Fishing at Siletz Bay near Lincoln City. *Photo by Terry Fisher.*

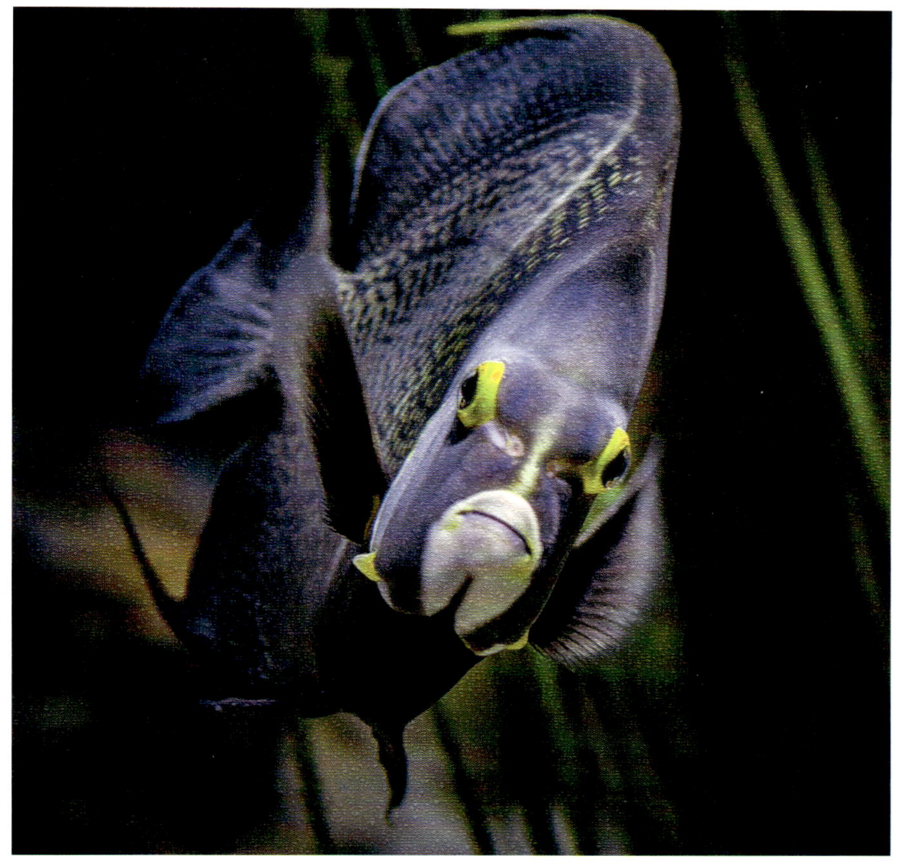

French angelfish at Newport Aquarium. *Photo by Judy Benson LaNier.* 51

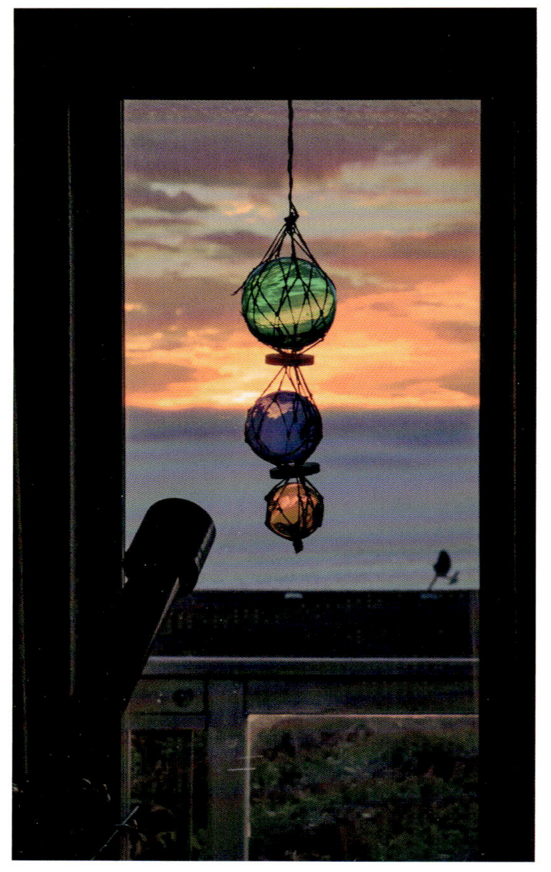

52   Glass floats and sunset in Brookings. *Photo by Graham Lewis.*

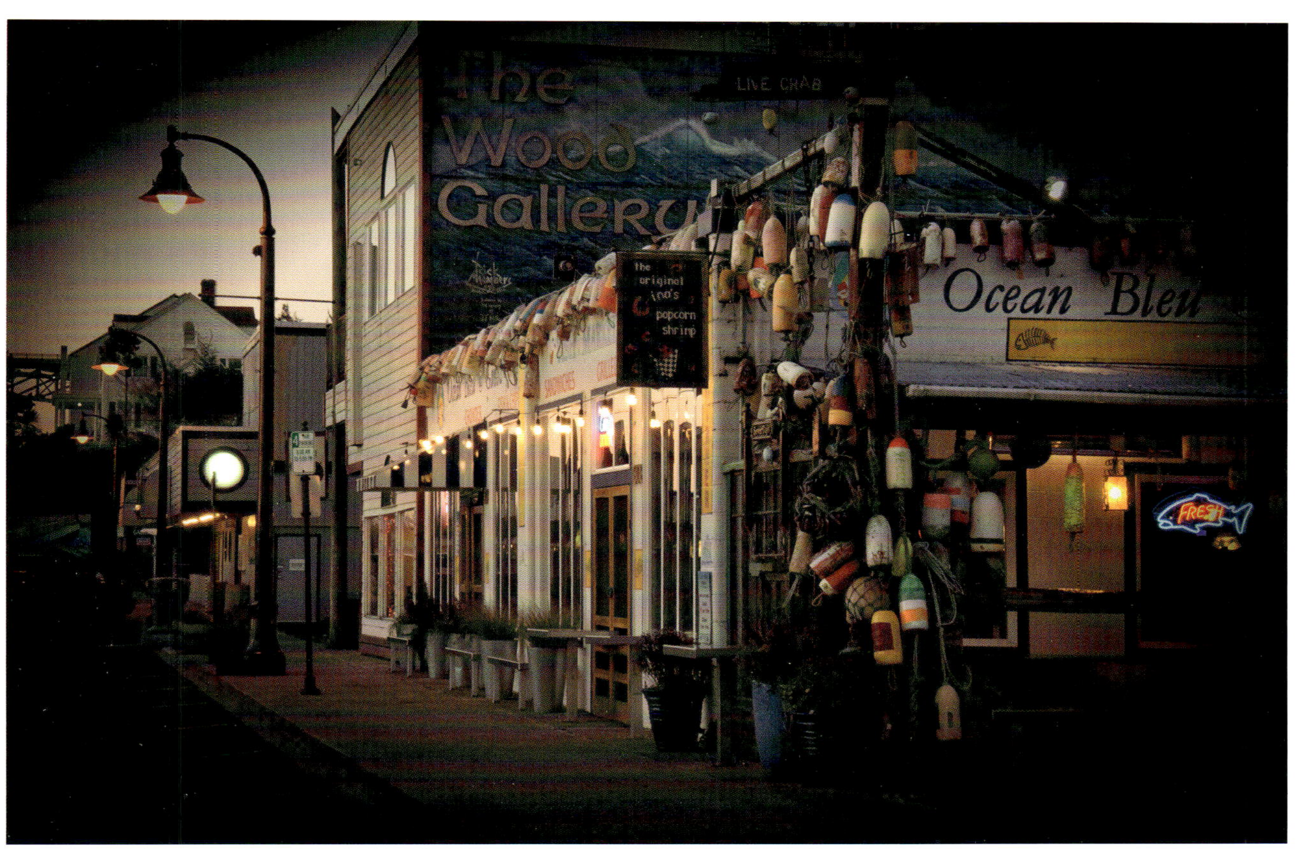

Newport at night. *Photo by Marilyn Dierks.*   53

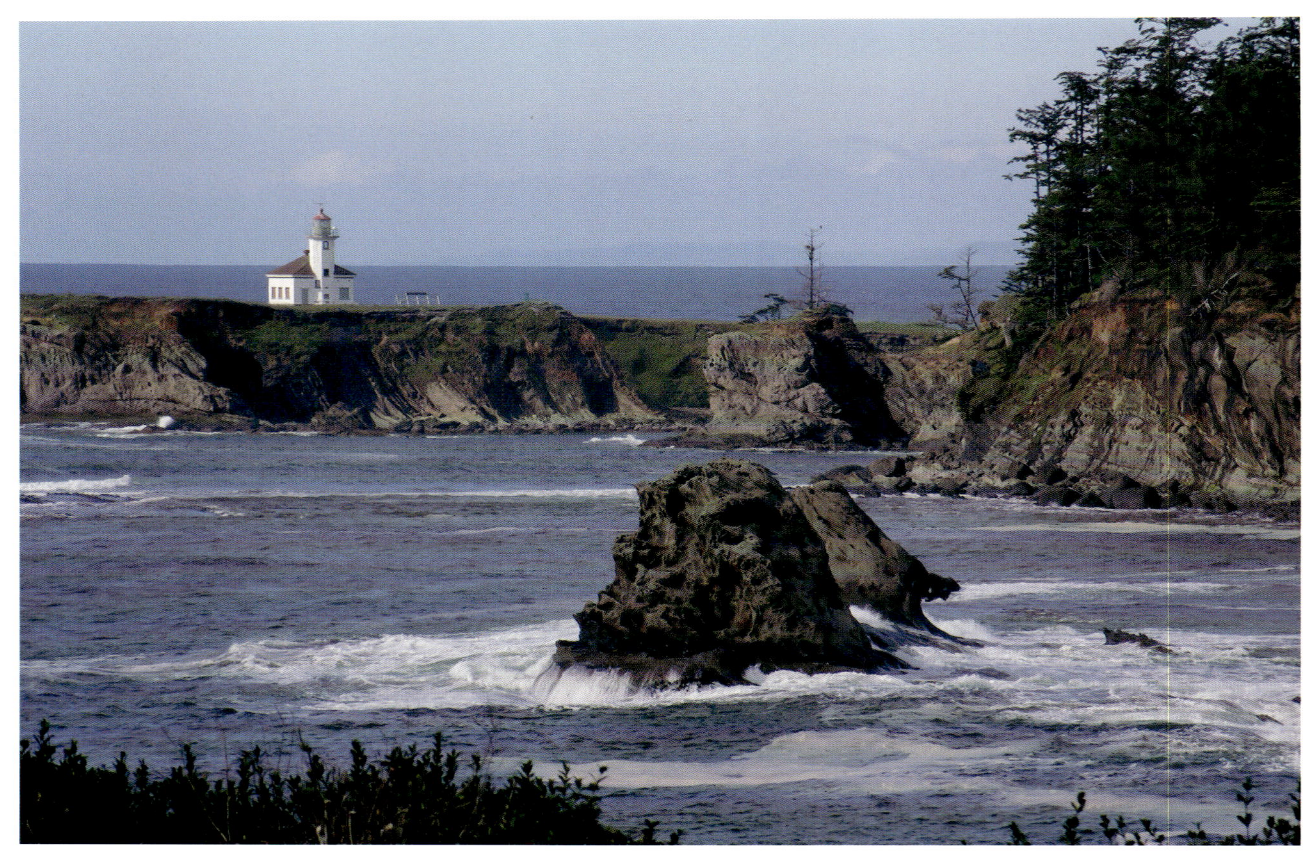

   Cape Arago Lighthouse. *Photo by Ken Deveney.*

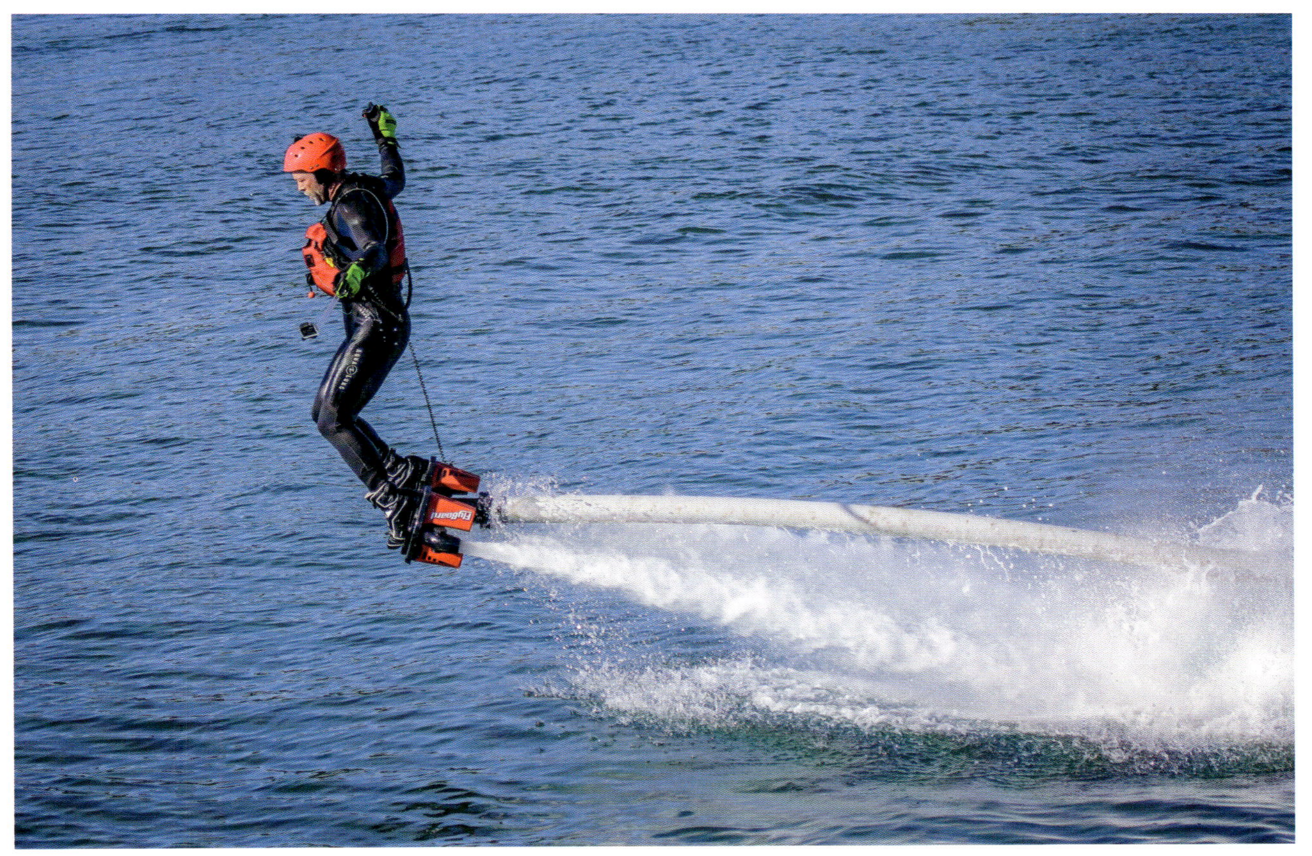

Hydroflying in Brookings. *Photo by Terry Fisher.*   55

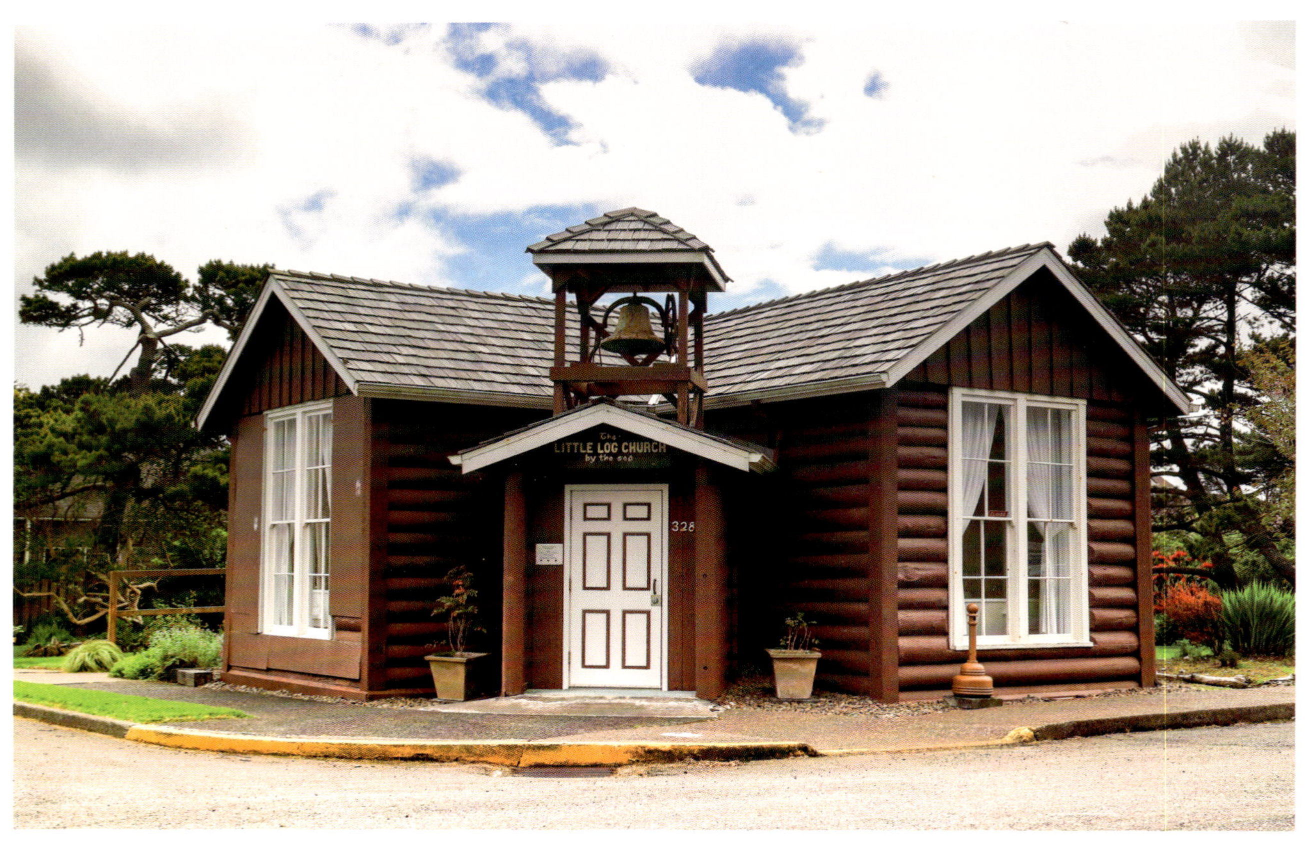

Little Log Church Museum, Yachats. Assembled in the 1920s by community volunteers,
 it was built using local timber hauled down the Yachats River. *Photo by Terry Fisher.*

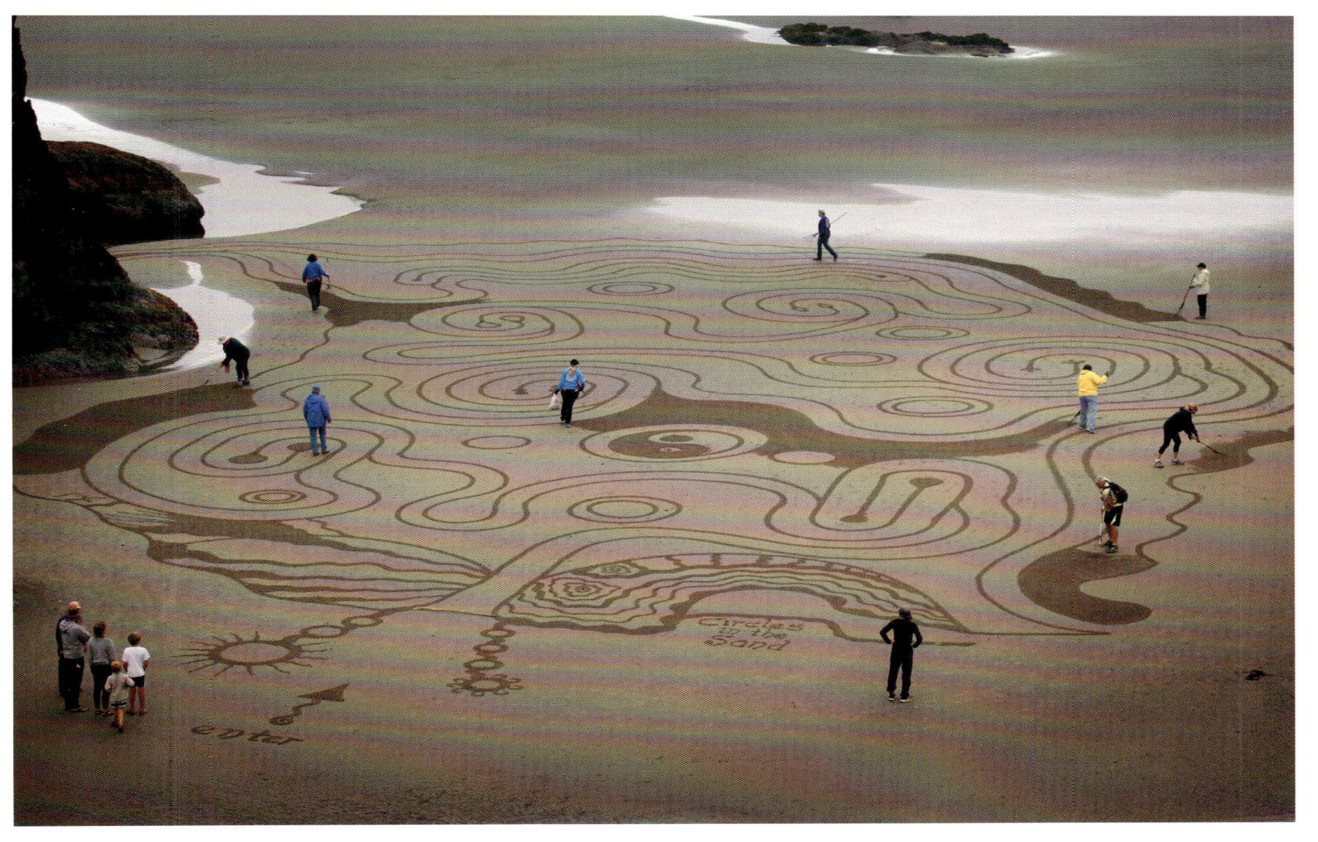

Circles in the sand, Bandon. Created and designed by Denny Dyke, this unique, albeit temporary, labyrinth art event draws hundreds of volunteers and visitors to the sand near Face Rock. *Photo by John Kirk.*

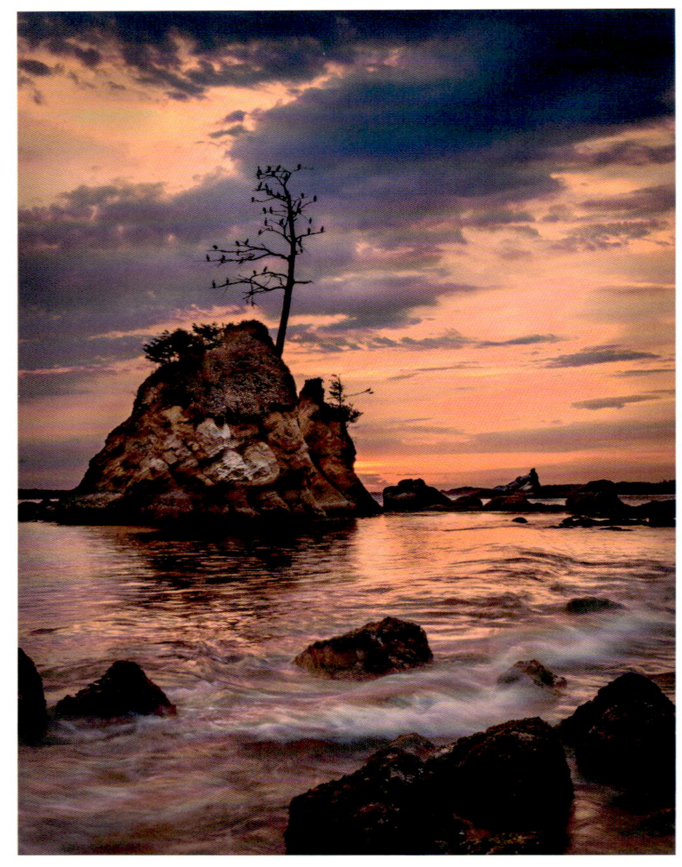

58   Sunset in Tillamook Bay at Garibaldi. *Photo by Rudy Dierks.*

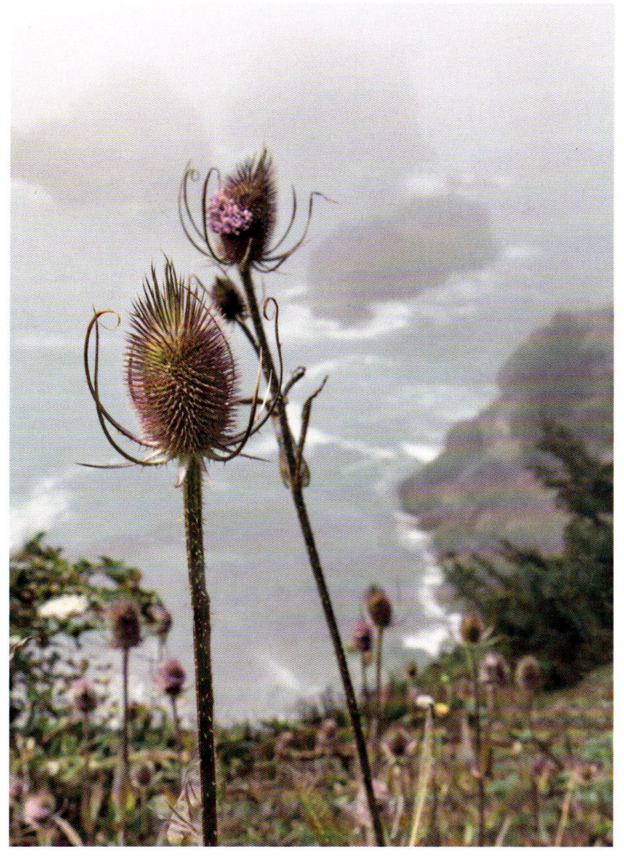

Thistles above the coastline. *Photo by Sue Stendebach.*

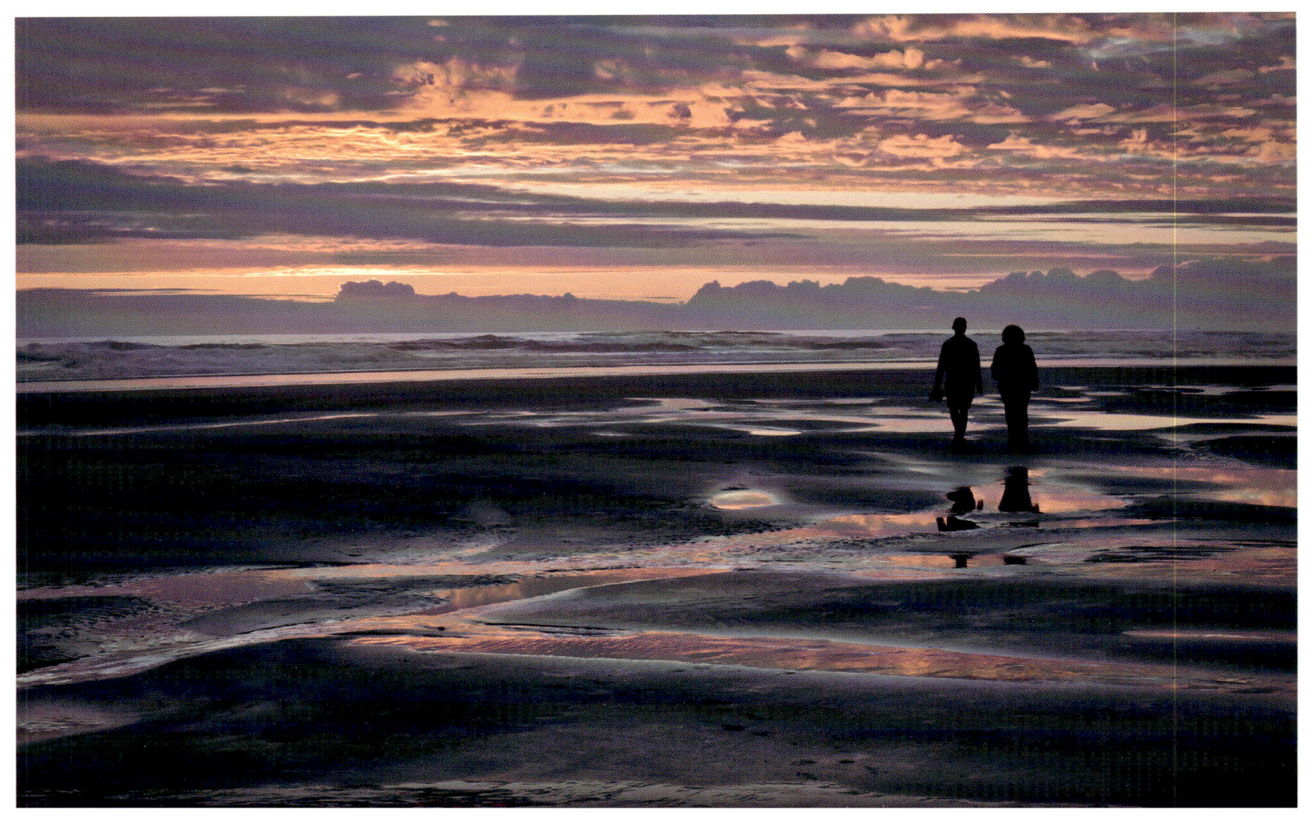

60   Manzanita Beach. *Photo by Kate Geary.*

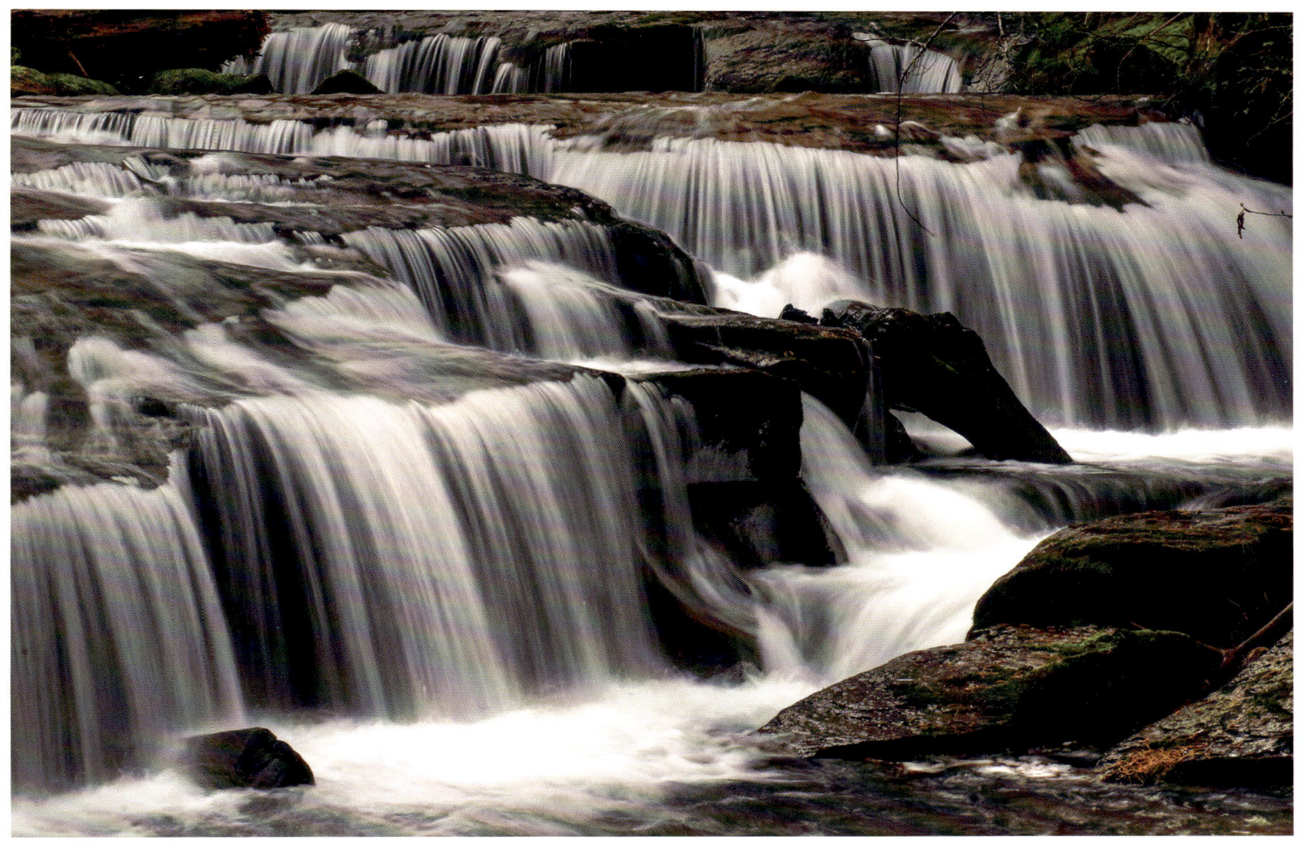

Sweet Creek Falls is fifteen miles east of Florence. *Photo by Jay Newman.*

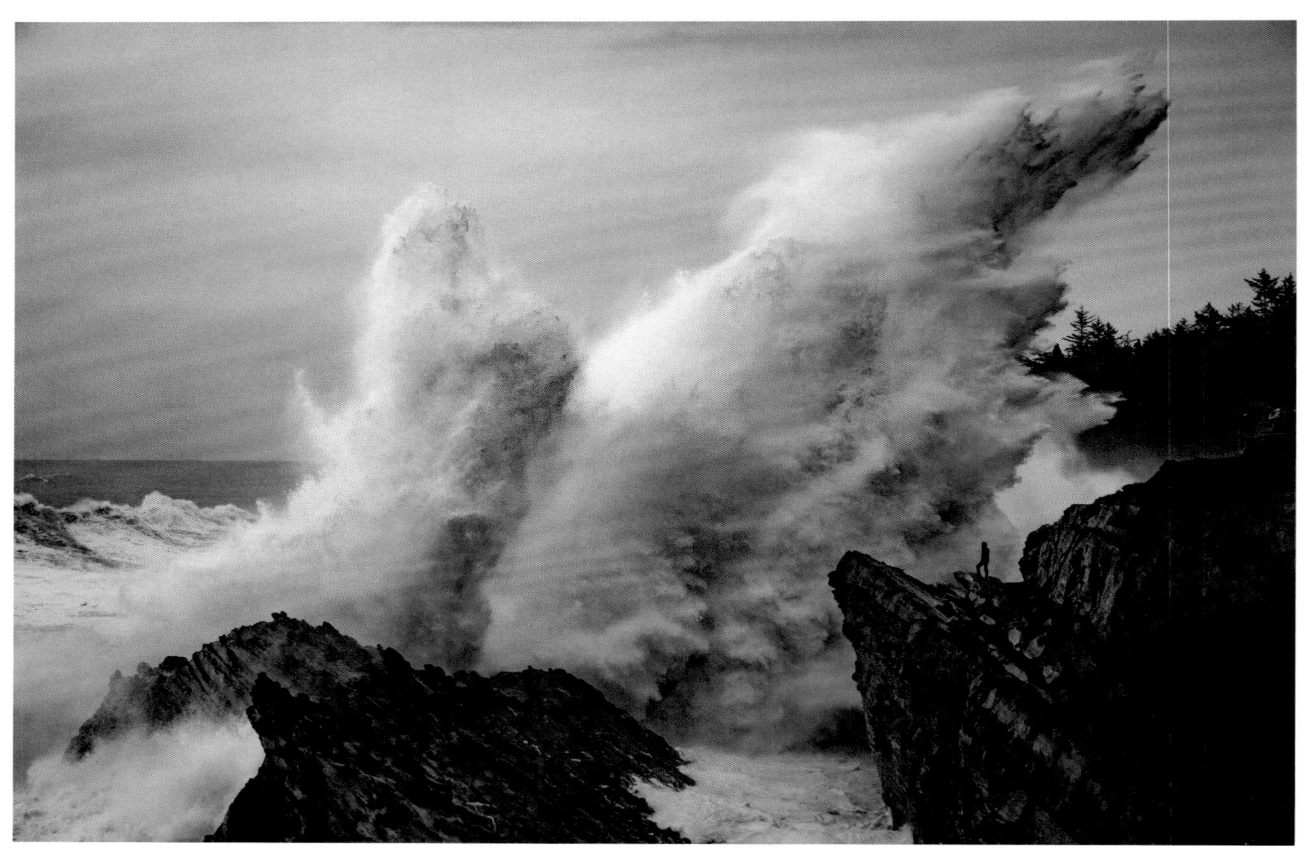

 Shore Acres' powerful waves. *Photo by Vldn Taylor.*

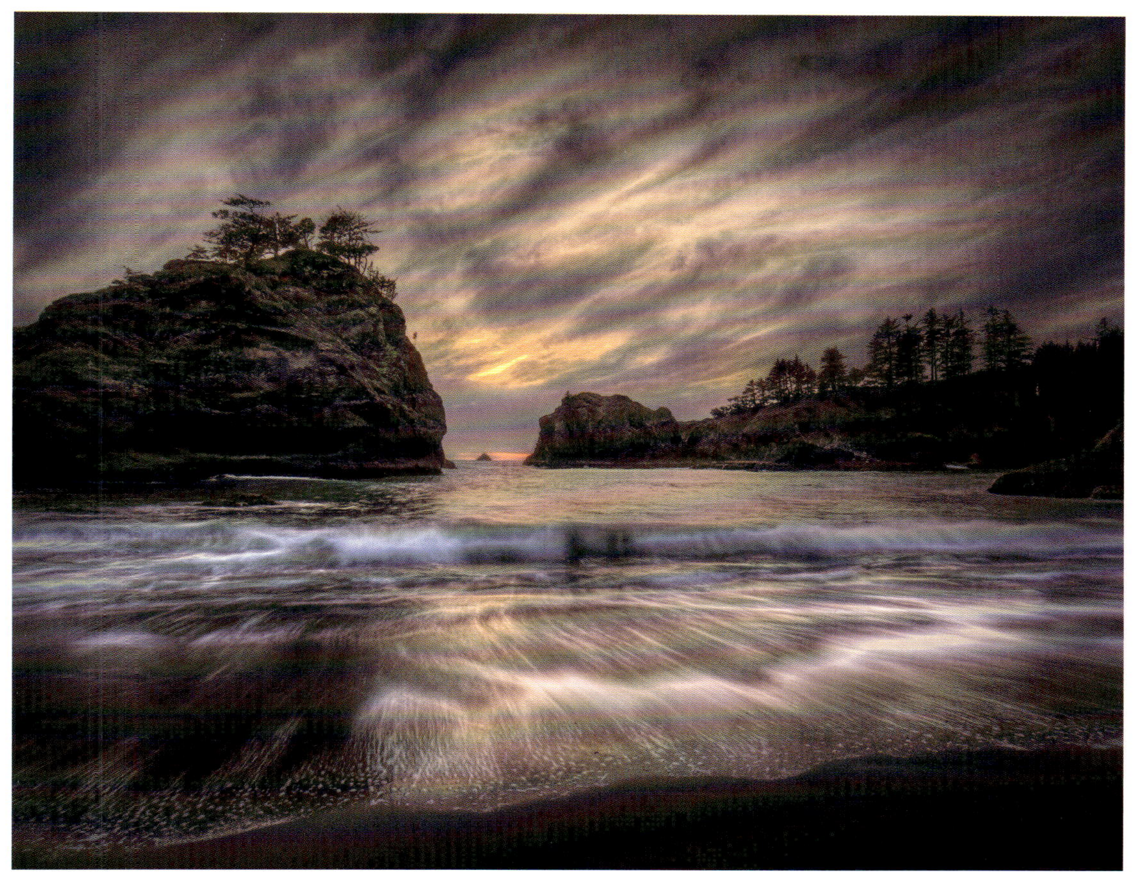

Secret Beach. *Photo by Rudy Dierks.*   63

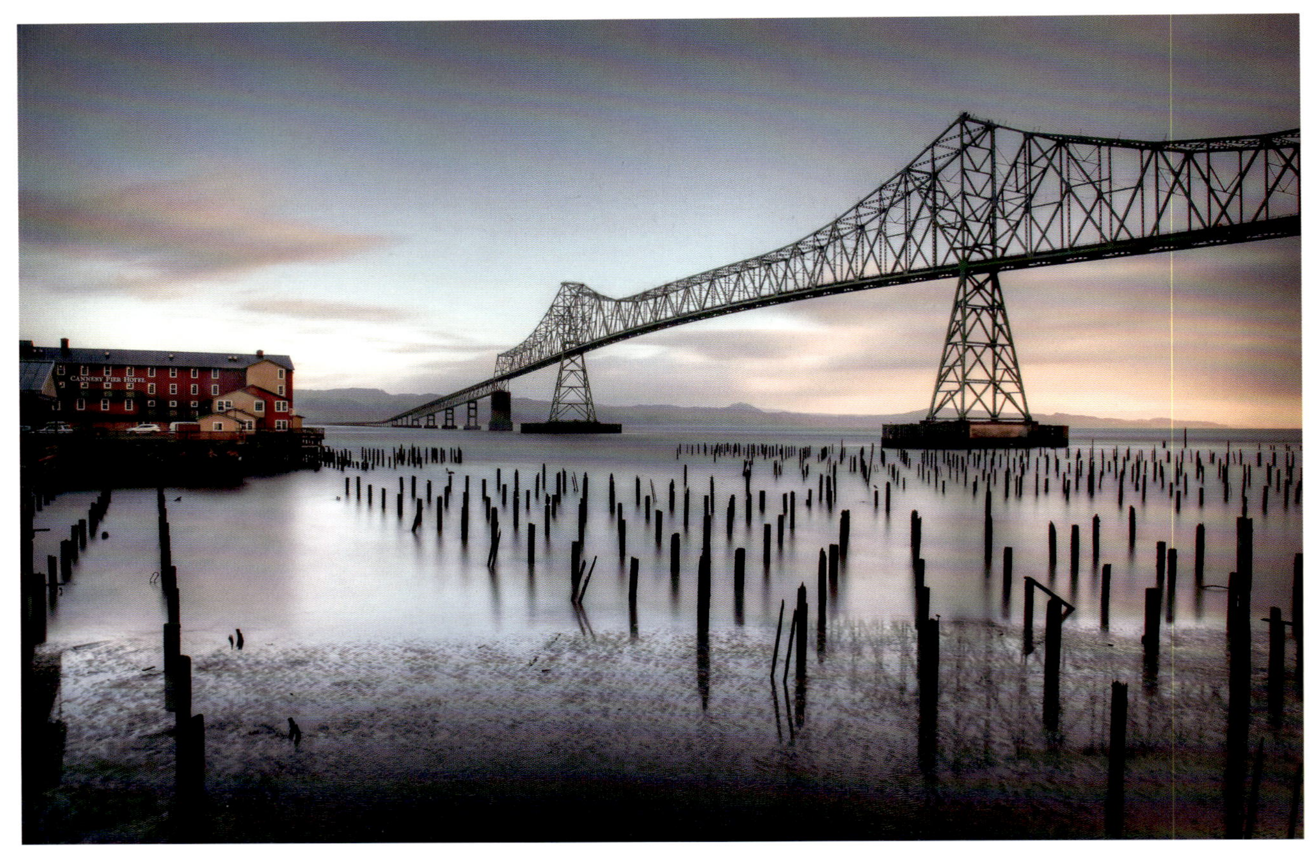

  Astoria-Megler Bridge. *Photo by John Kirk.*

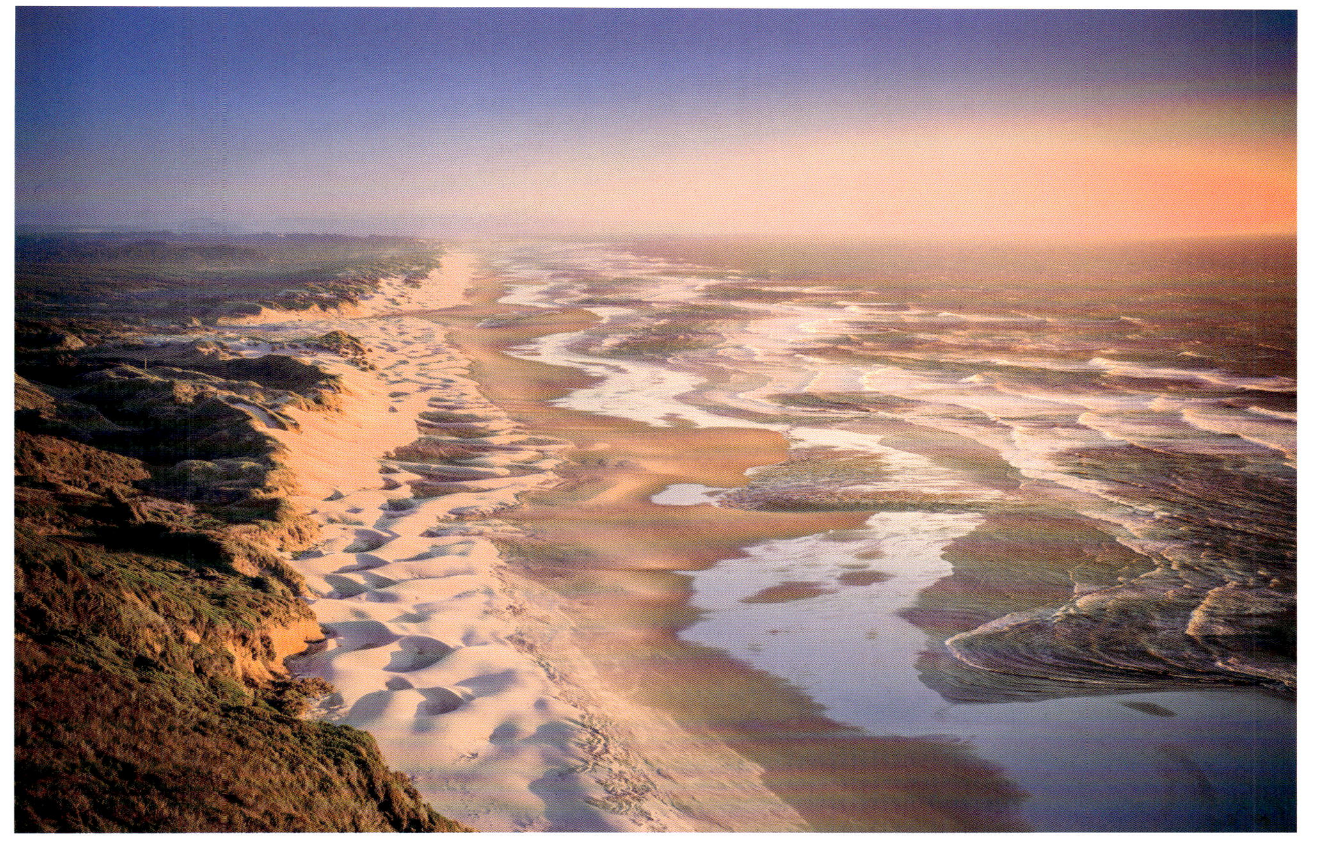

Highway 101 Coastline north of Florence. *Photo by Brandon Herring.*

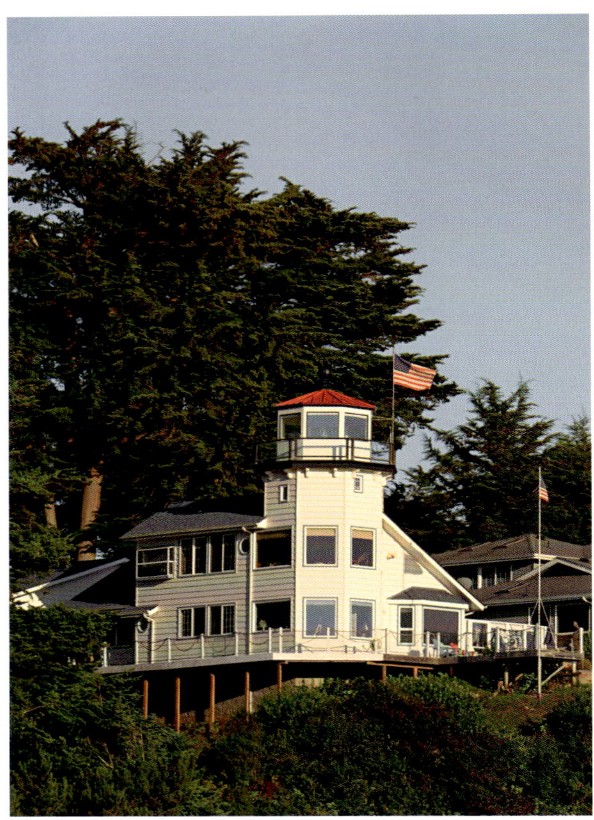

Pelican Bay Lighthouse, Brookings. One of two privately owned lighthouses in Oregon, it was first lit in 1997 and stands 141 feet above sea level. *Photo by Barbara Tricarico.*

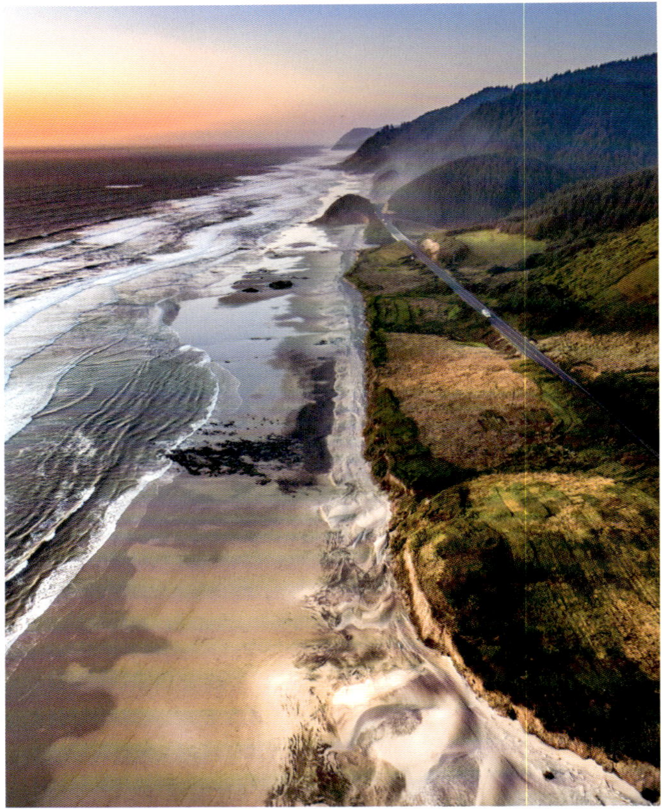

Coastline north of Florence. *Photo by Brandon Herring.*

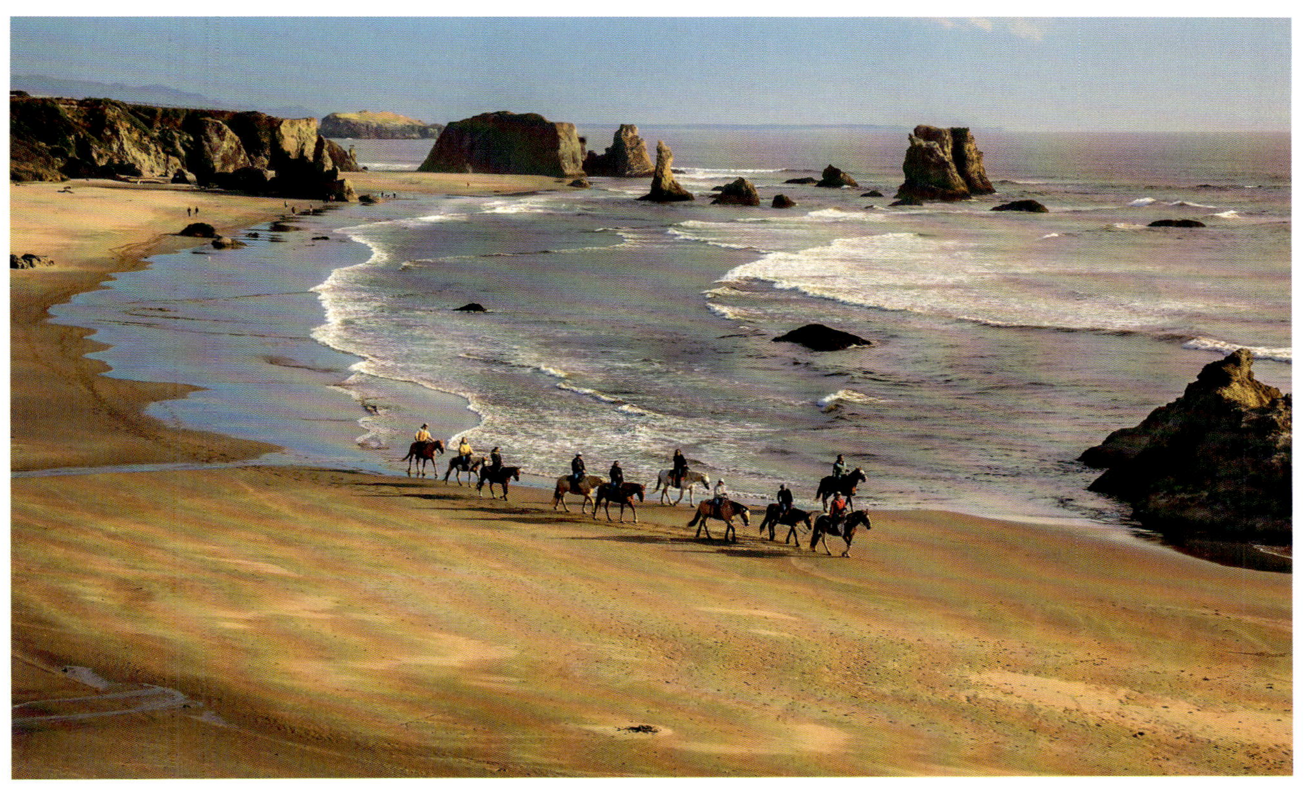

Horseback riding at Bandon Beach. *Photo by Neal R. Thompson.* 67

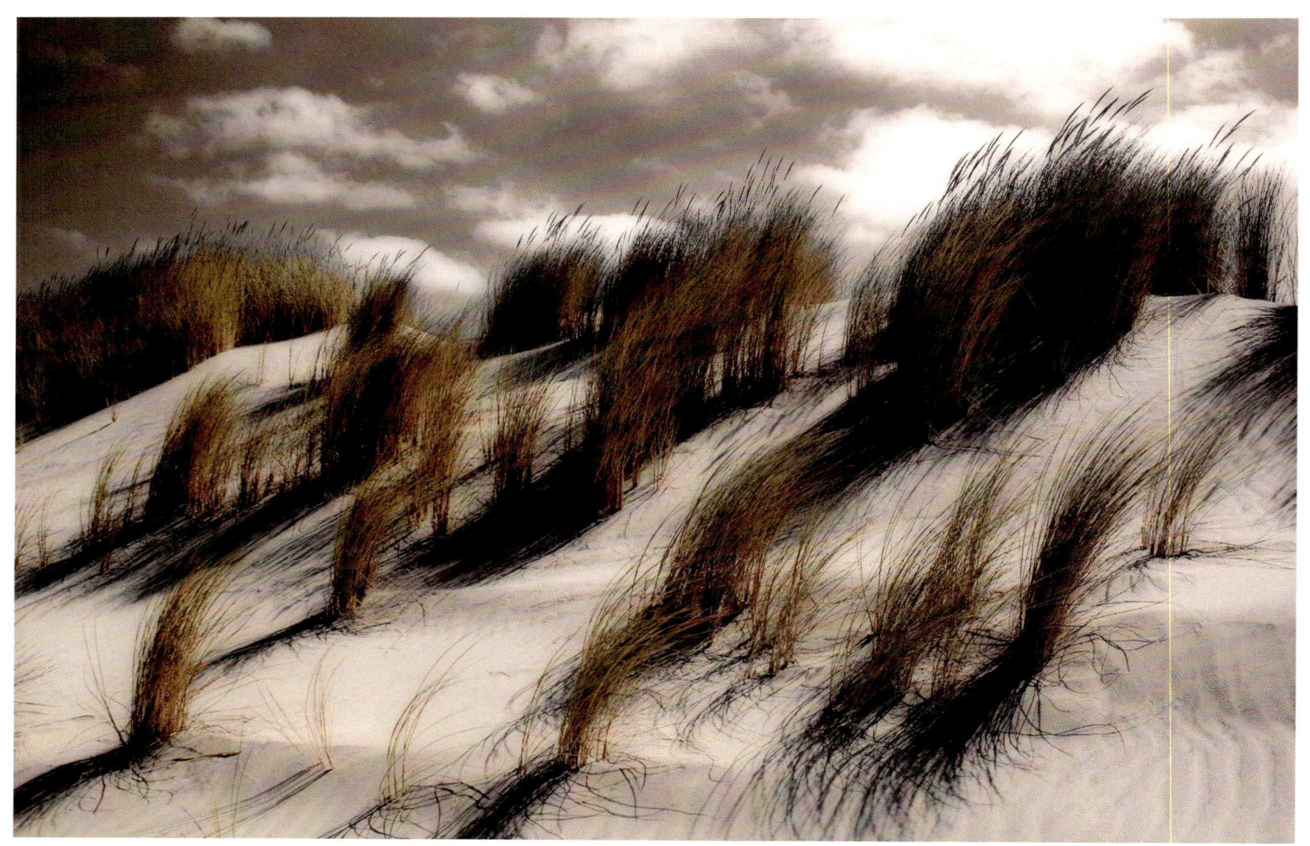

68   Dune grass. *Photo by David Lorenz Winston.*

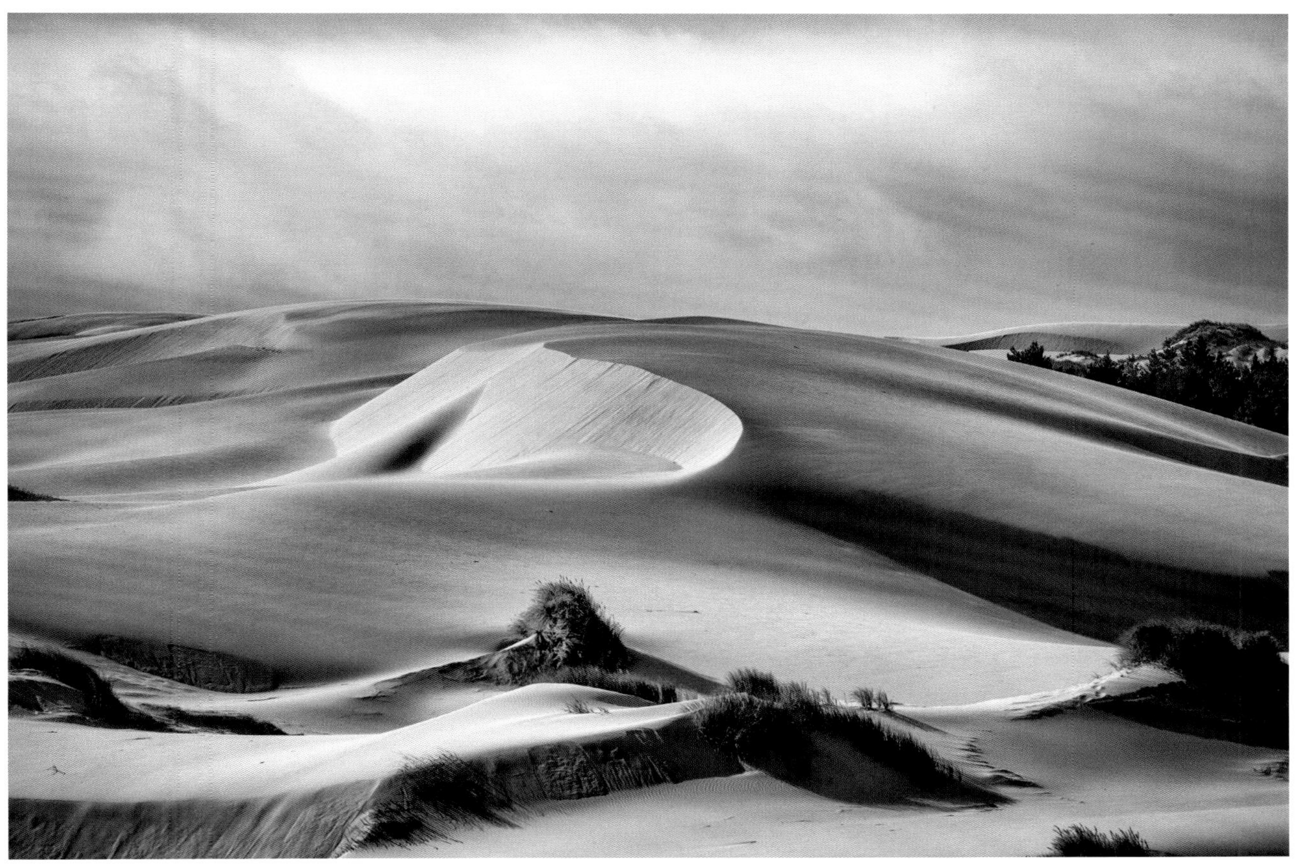

Oregon Dunes. *Photo by Kate Geary.*   69

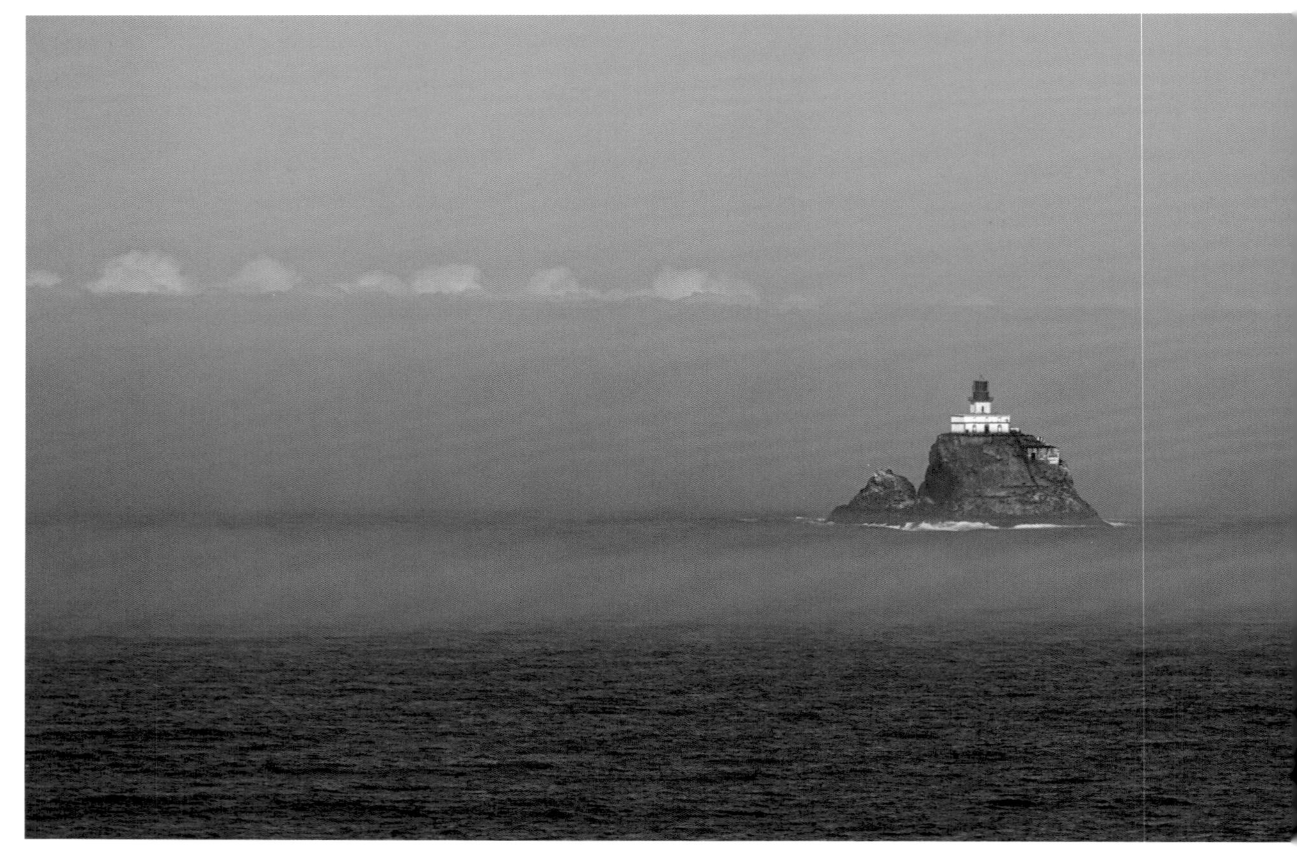

"Terrible Tilly" is the nickname for Tillamook Rock Lighthouse, built in 1881 and decommissioned in 1957. It sits one mile off the coast from Tillamook Head between Seaside and Cannon Beach and can be viewed from Ecola State Park. *Photo by Mason Marsh.*

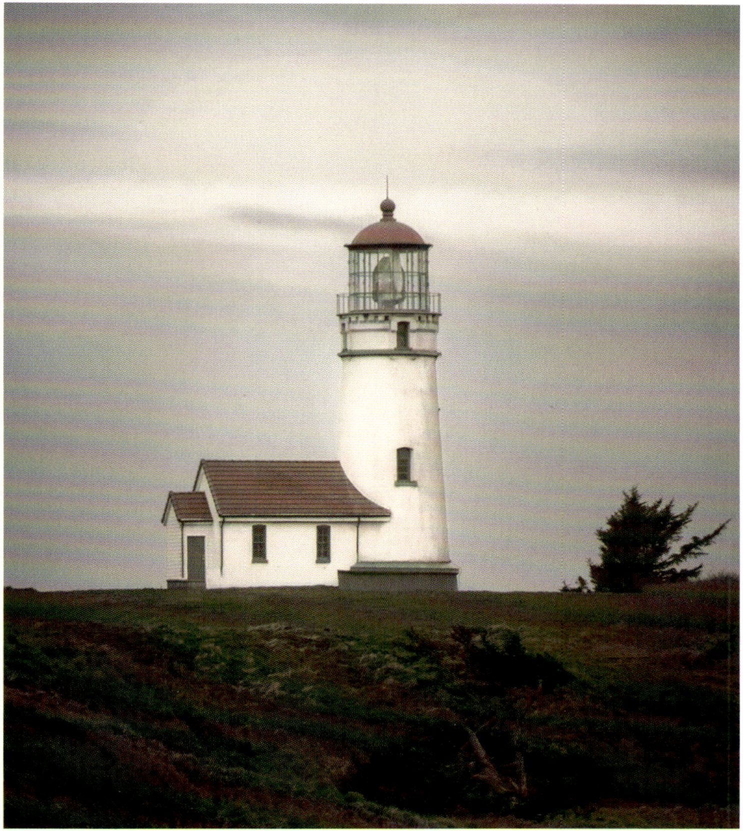

Cape Blanco Lighthouse opened in 1870 in Port Orford. Oregon's most westerly light, it has the highest focal plane above the sea (256 feet) and in 1903 welcomed Oregon's first woman keeper, Mabel E. Bretherton. *Photo by Geri H. Mathewson.*

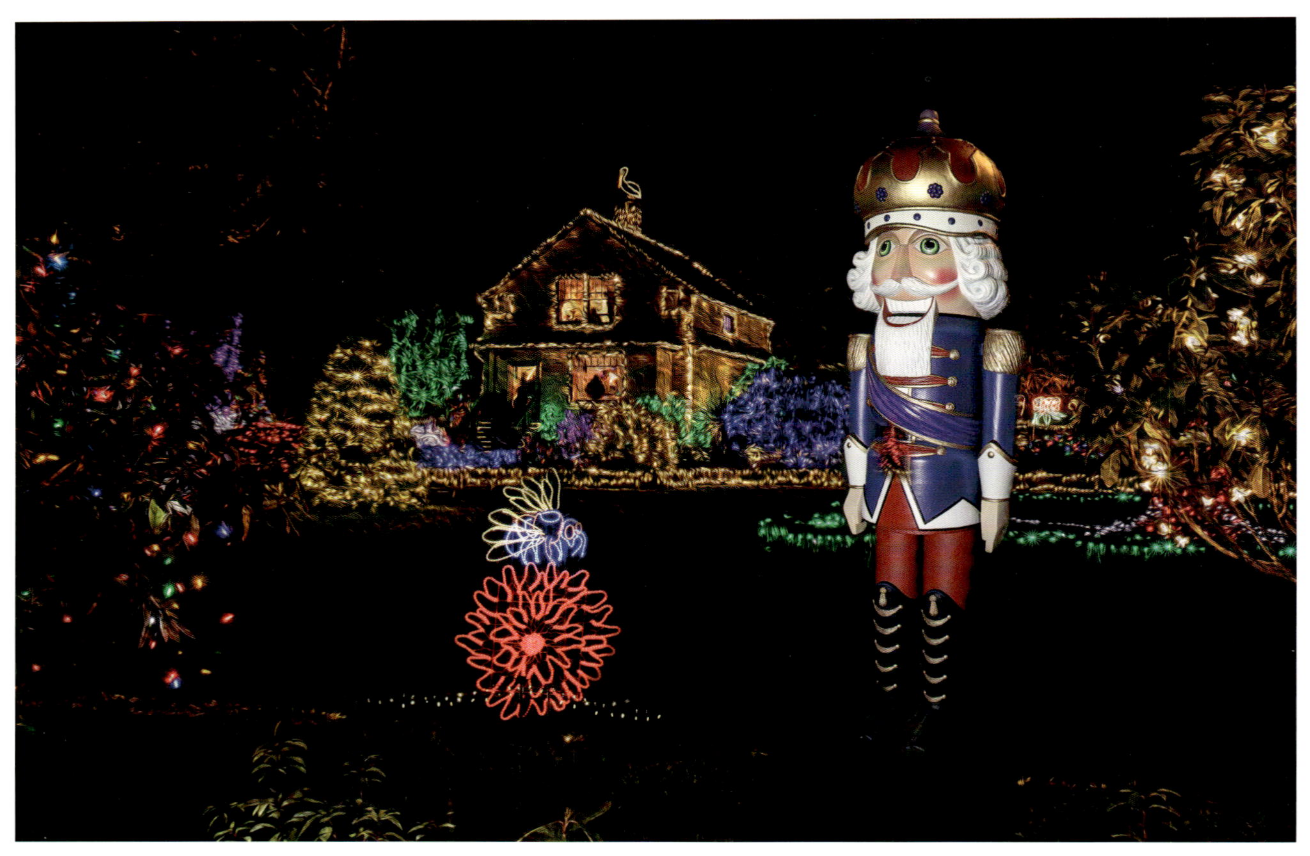

Holiday light display at Shore Acres. More than 325,000 LED lights adorn the grounds of Shore Acres between Thanksgiving Day and December 31. *Photo by Rudy Dierks.*

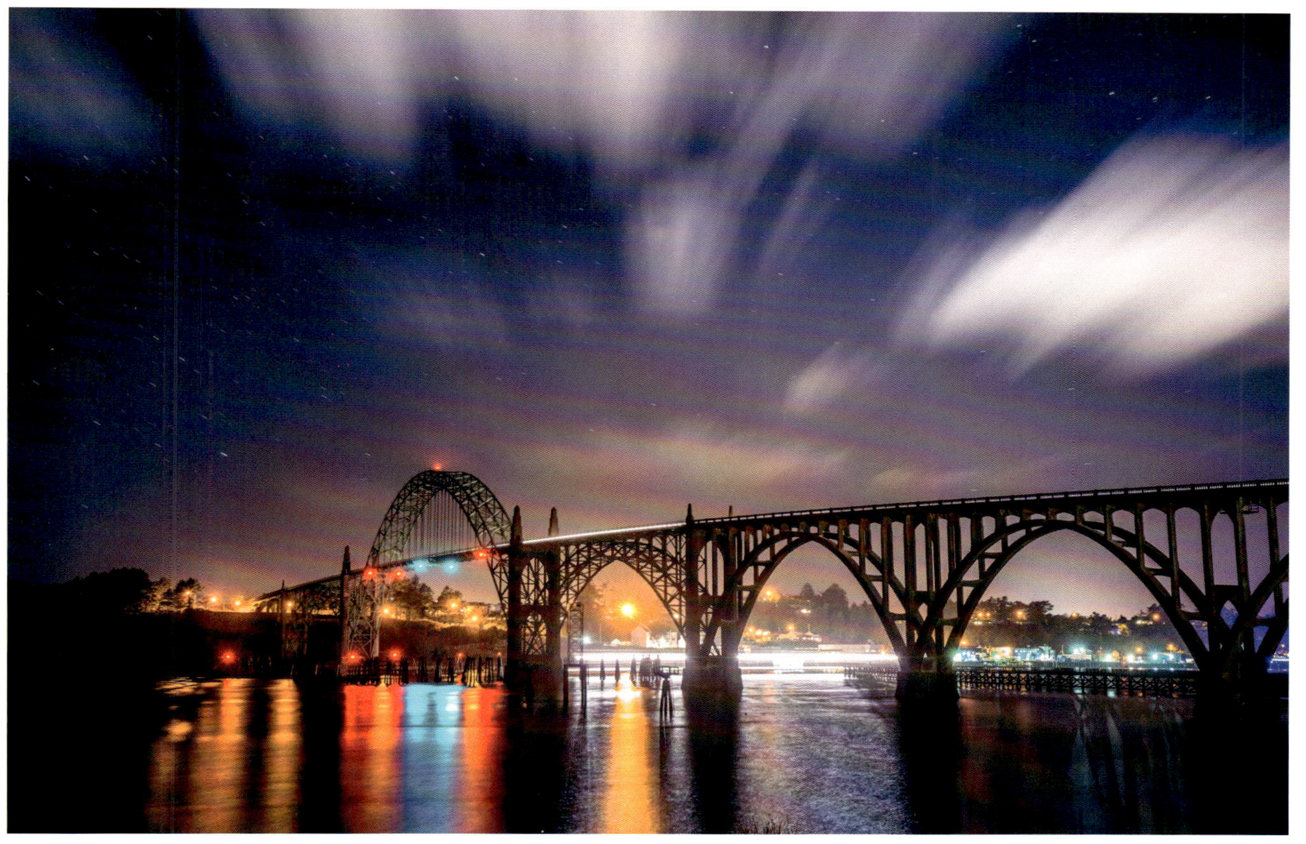

Yaquina Bay Bridge, Newport. The bridge opened in 1936. *Photo by Brandon Herring.*

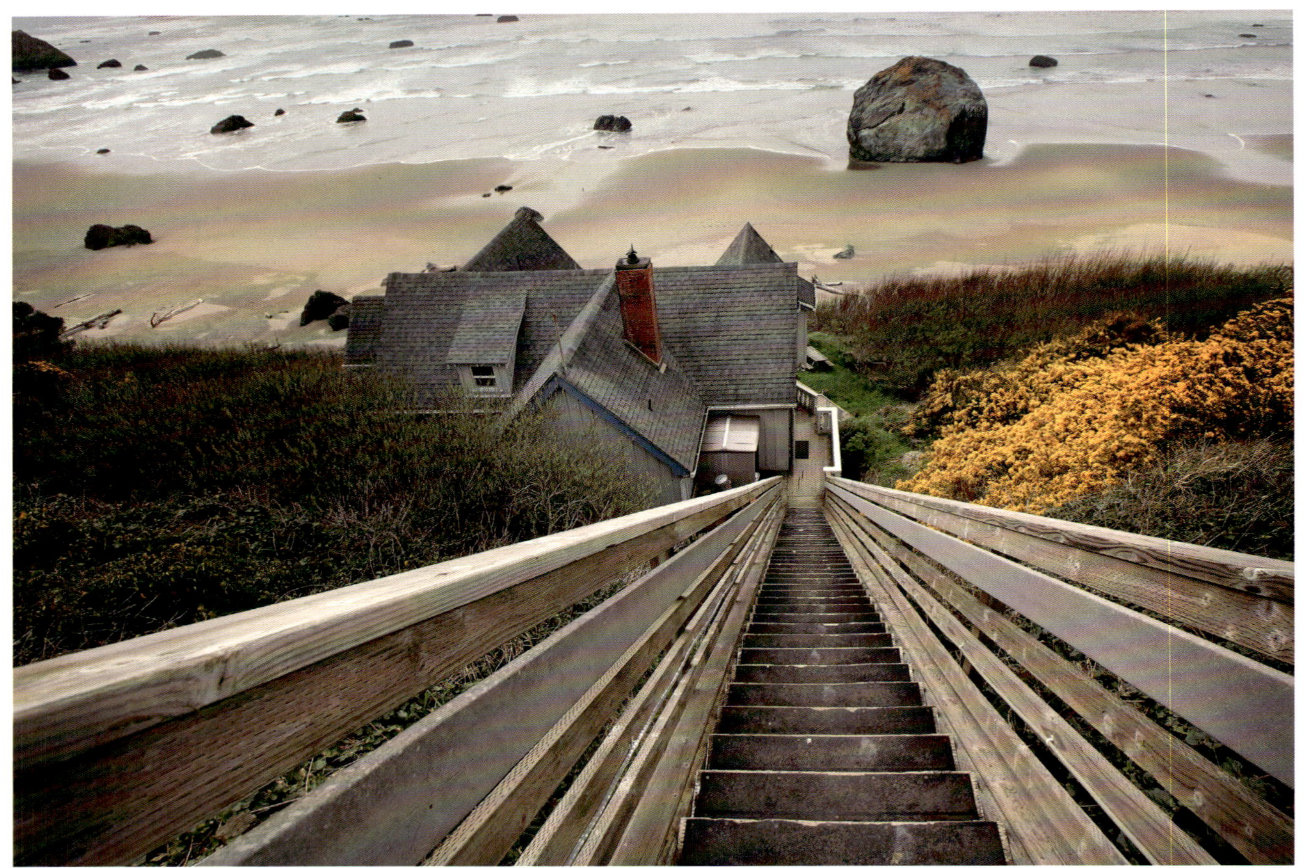

74   Bandon staircase. *Photo by John Kirk.*

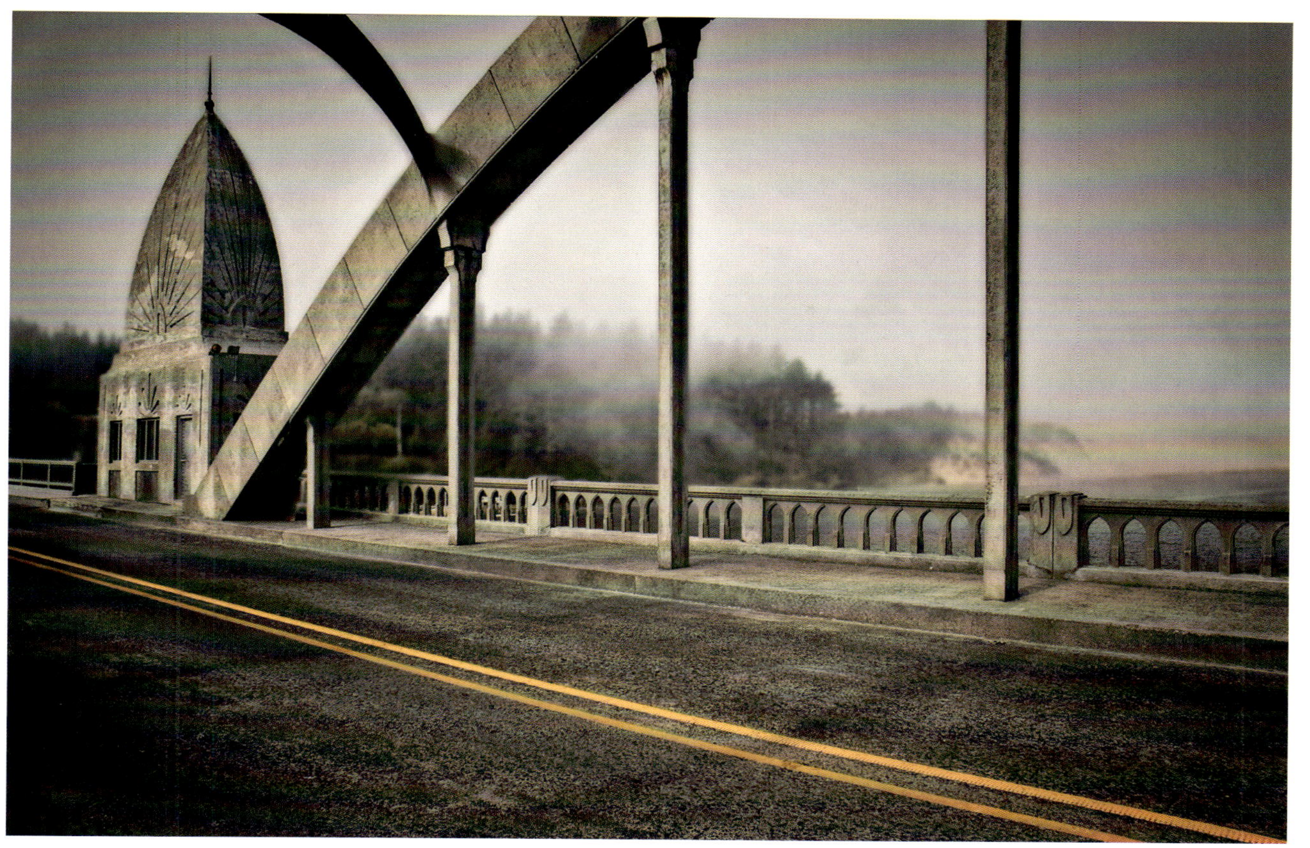

Siuslaw River Bridge. This art deco–inspired bridge opened in 1936. *Photo by David Lorenz Winston.*   75

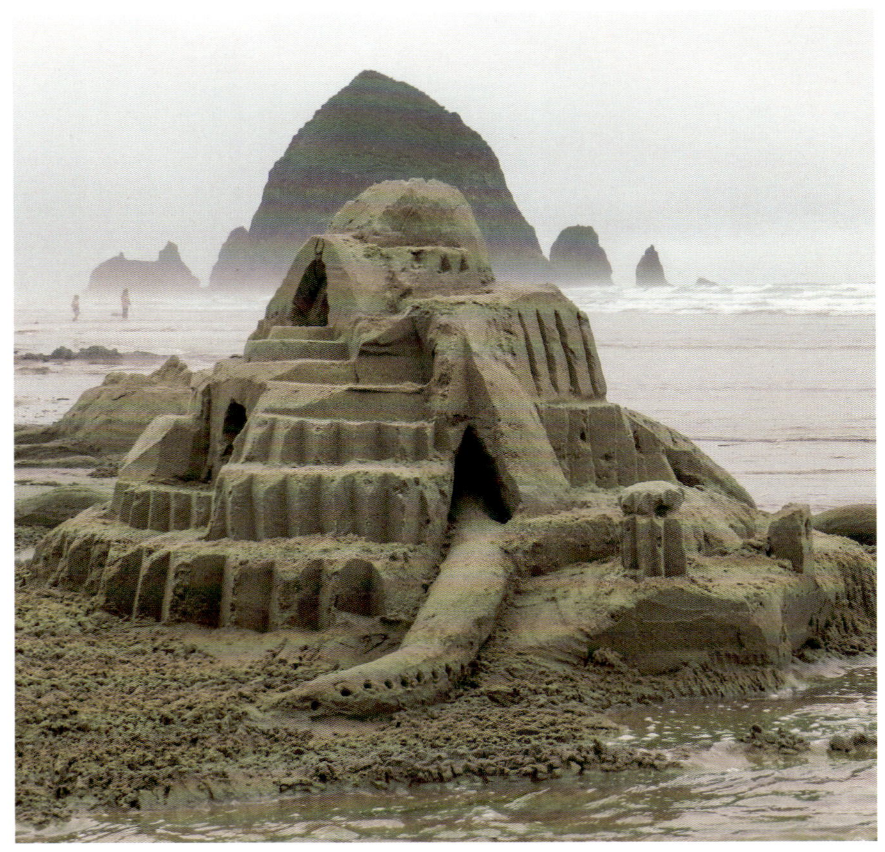

 Sand Castle Day at Cannon Beach. *Photo by Charles Hillestad.*

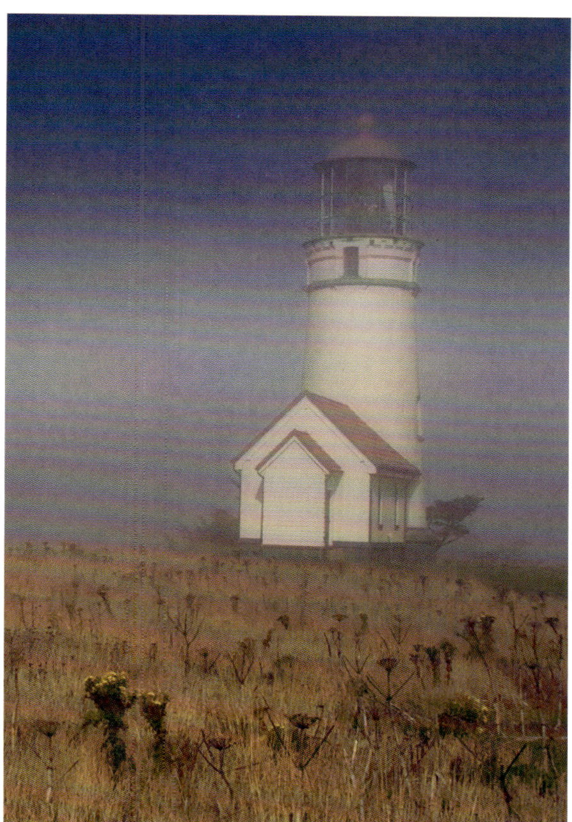

Umpqua River Lighthouse, Winchester Bay. First lit in 1857, the original lighthouse was prone to flooding. A new light was built in 1892 with the same plans as the Heceta Head Light. *Photo by David Lorenz Winston.*

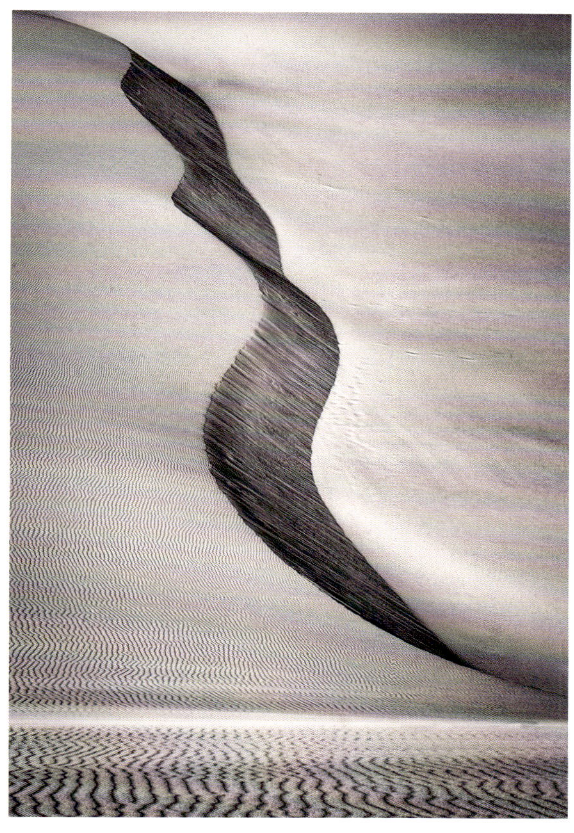

Wind-etched dunes. *Photo by Kate Geary.*

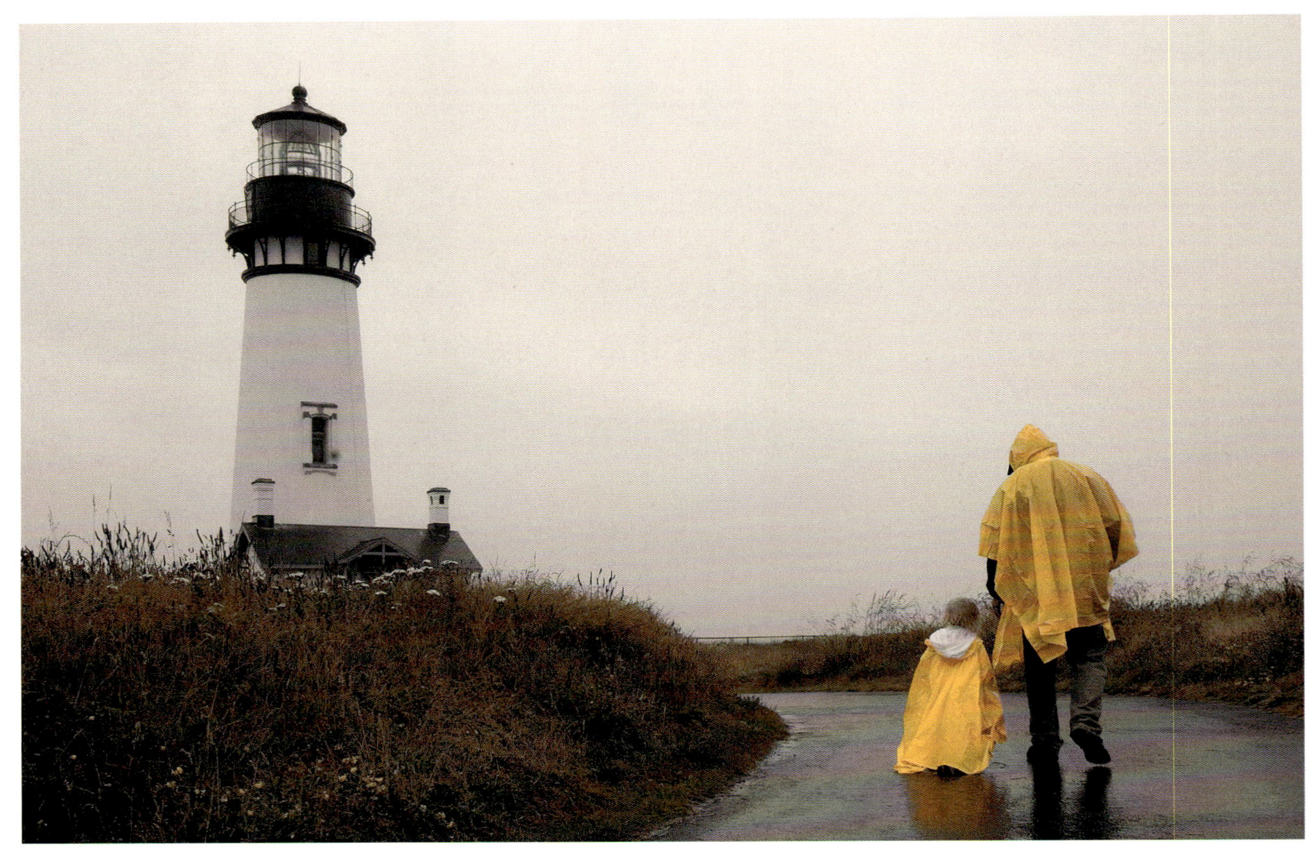

    Rainy day at Yaquina Head Lighthouse. *Photo by David Lorenz Winston.*

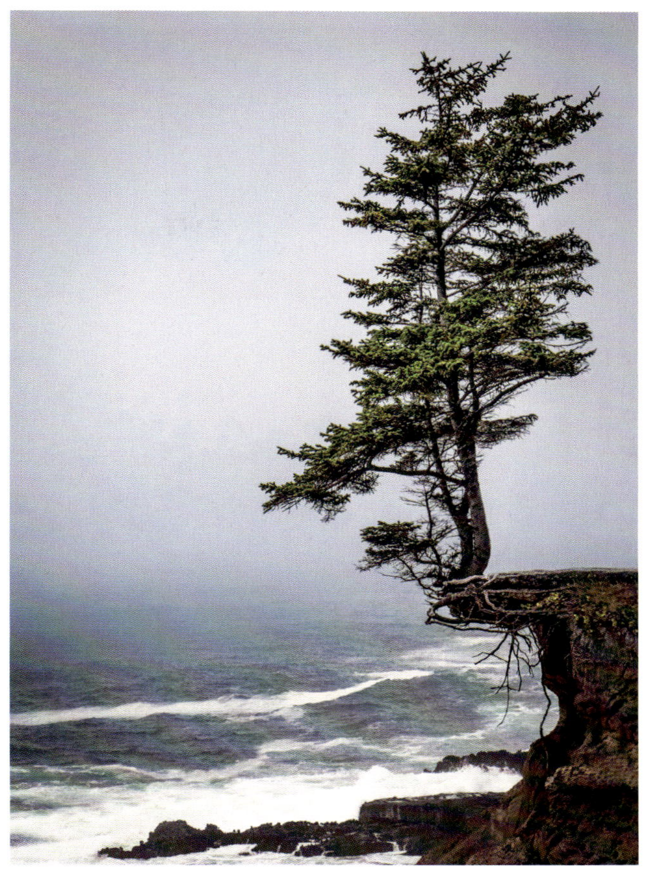

Perseverance at Shore Acres. *Photo by Sue Stendebach.*   79

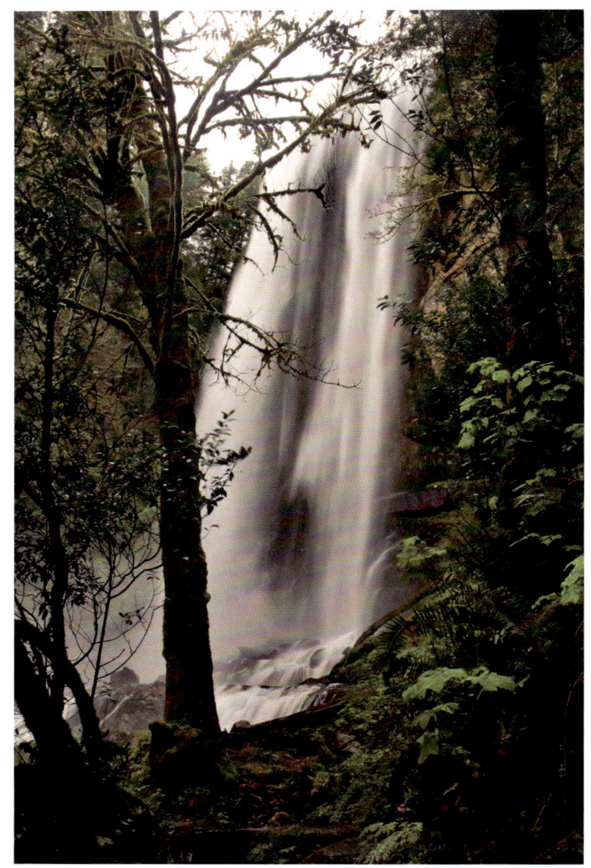

80   Silver Falls. *Photo by Jay Newman.*

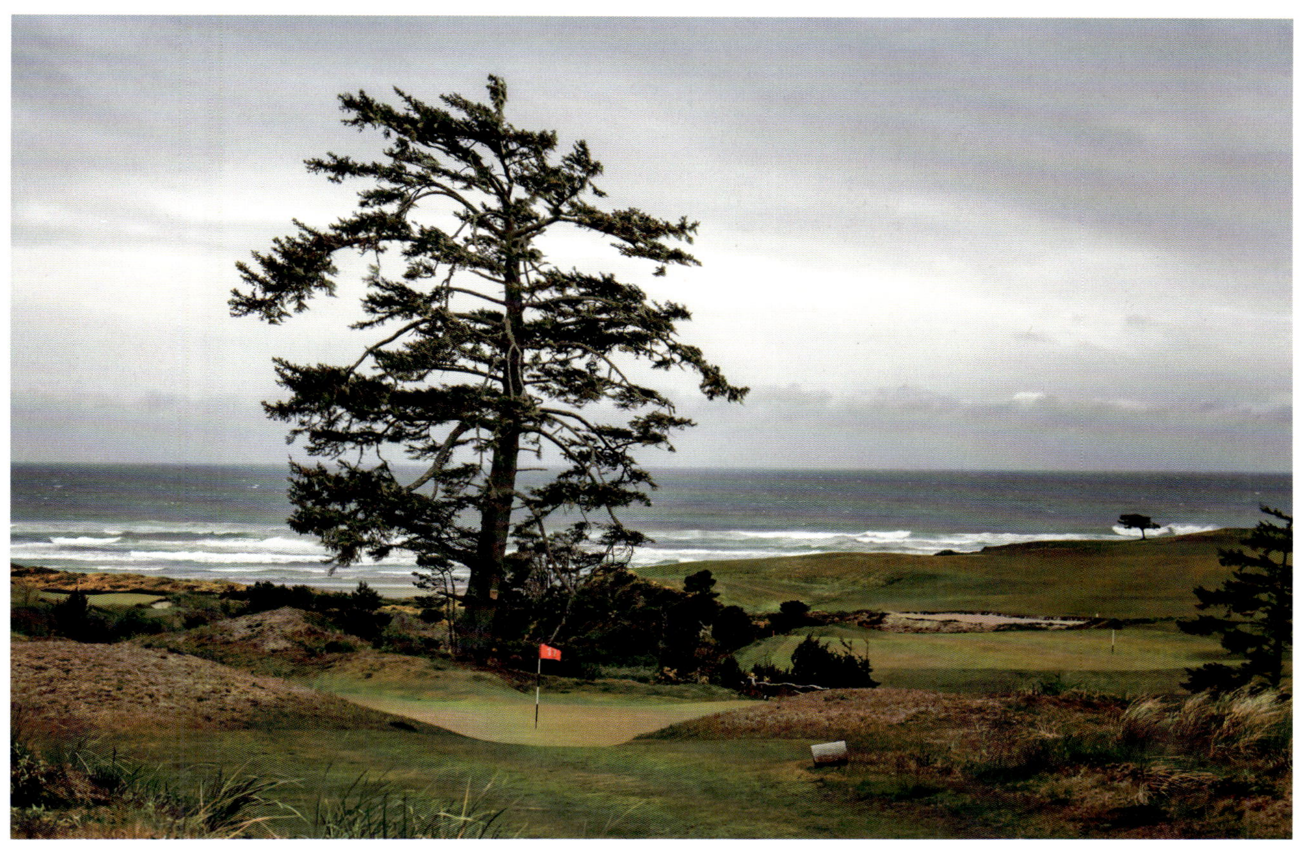

Bandon Dunes Golf Course is a world-class course perched 100 feet above the rugged coastline. *Photo by Barbara Tricarico.*

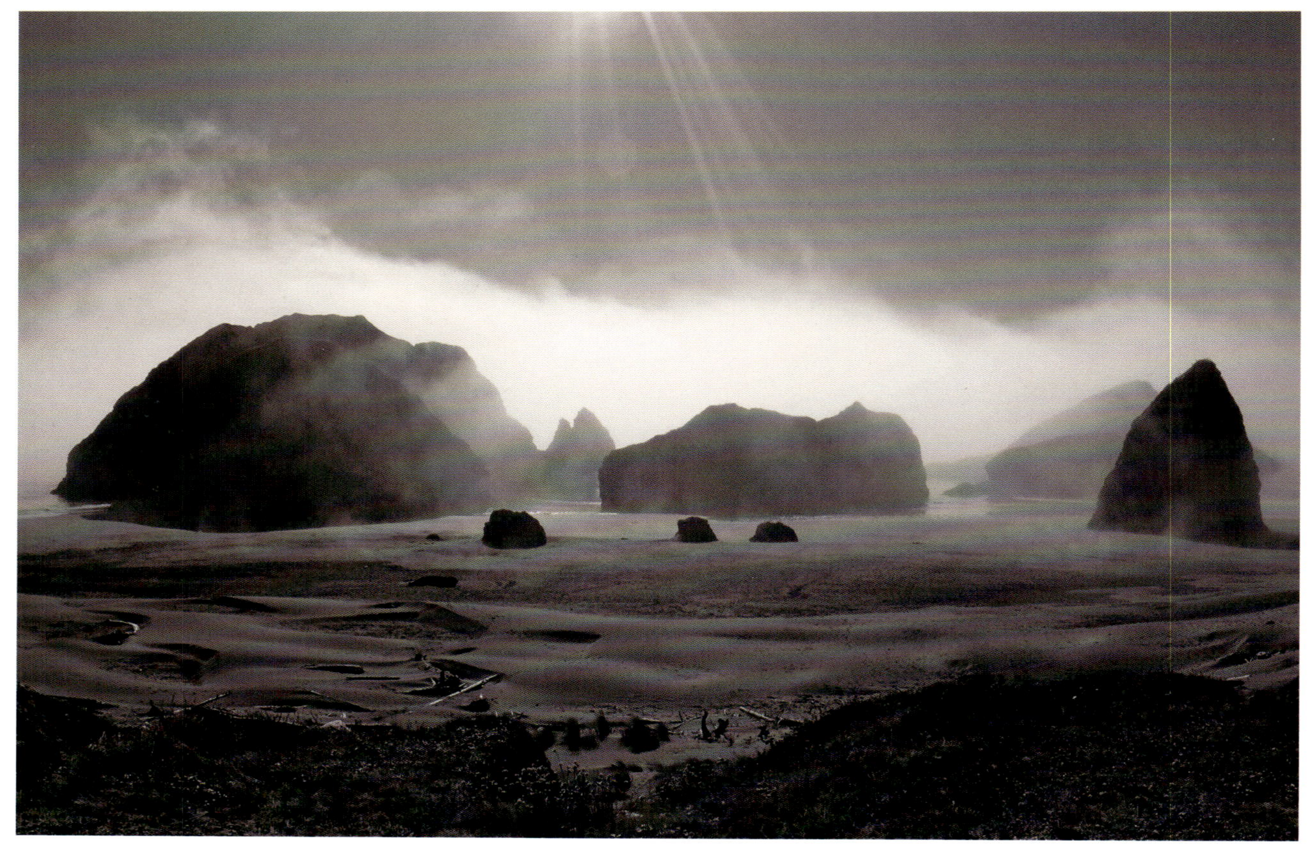

82   Meyers Creek Beach. *Photo by Sue Newman.*

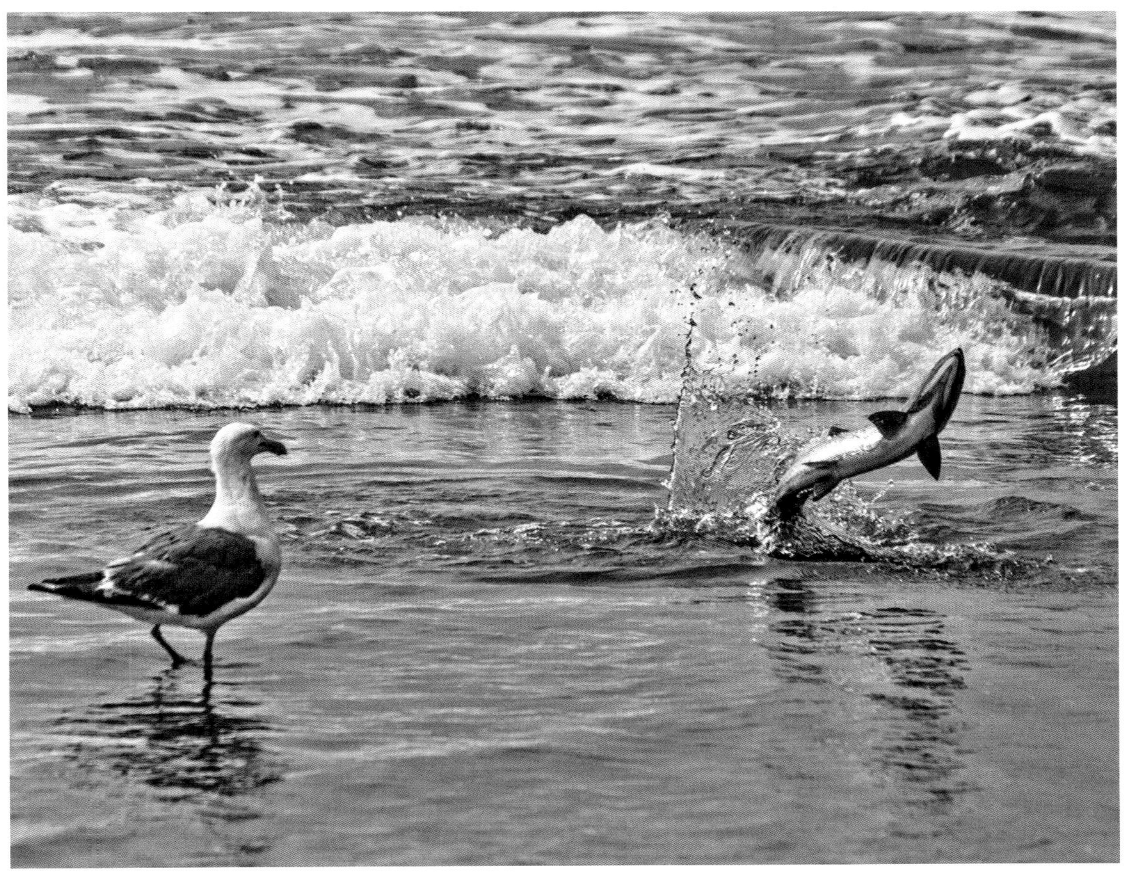

Seagull and salmon, Bandon. *Photo by George F. Peterson.*   83

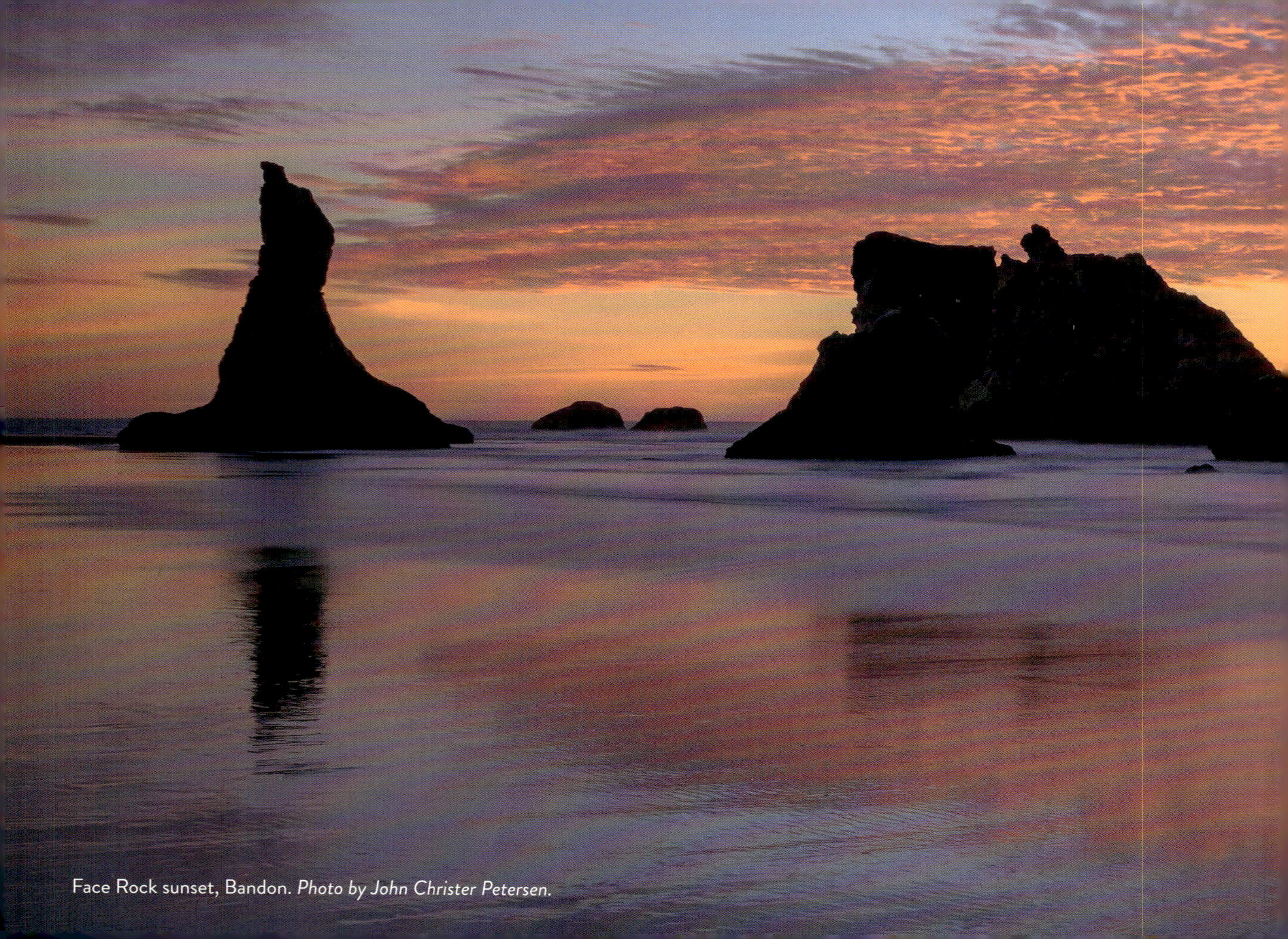

Face Rock sunset, Bandon. *Photo by John Christer Petersen.*

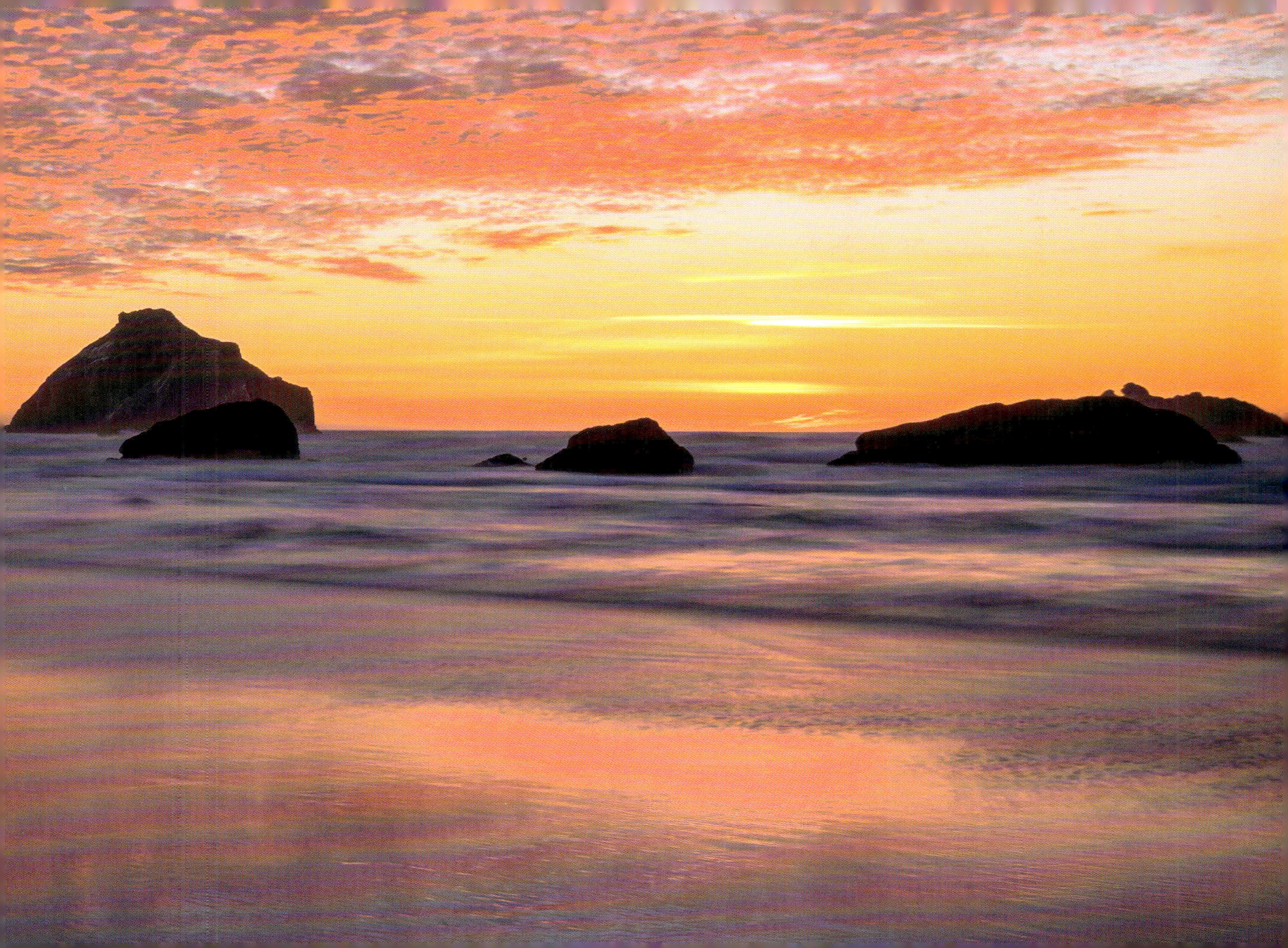

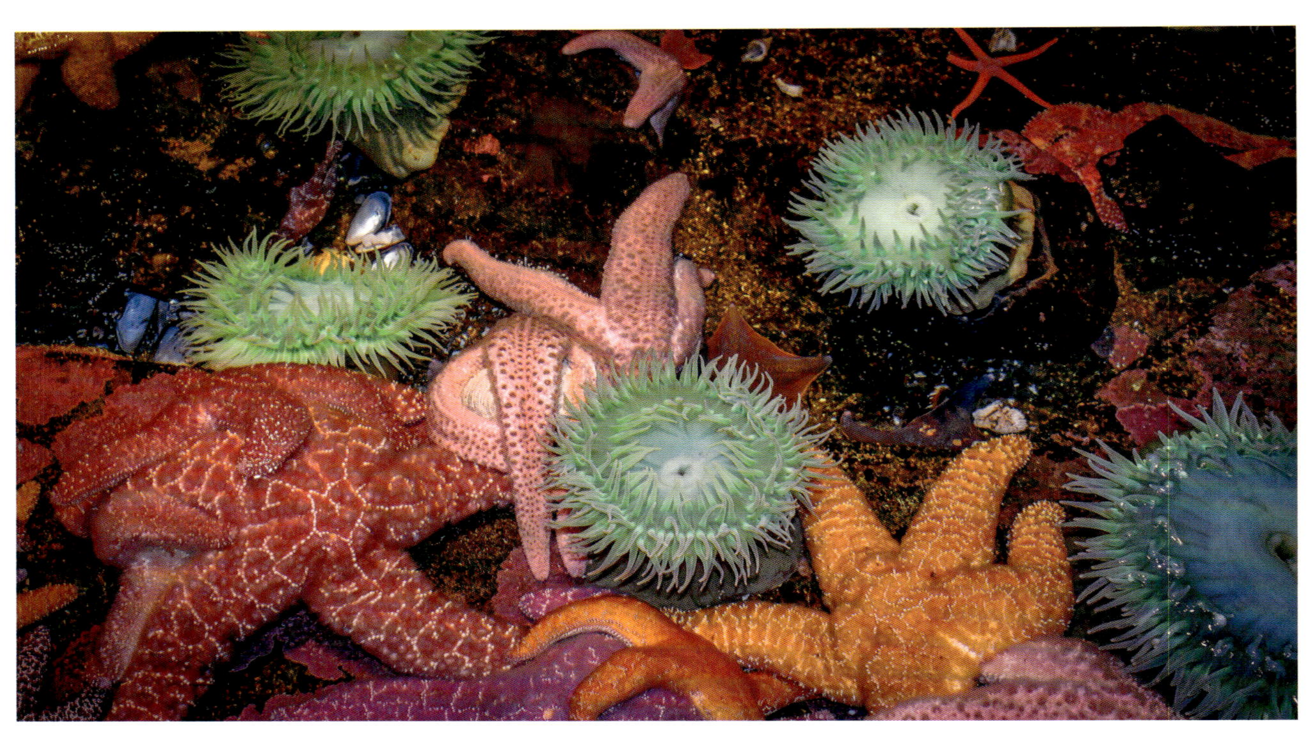

86   Tidal pool life, Bandon. *Photo by Ellen Ahern.*

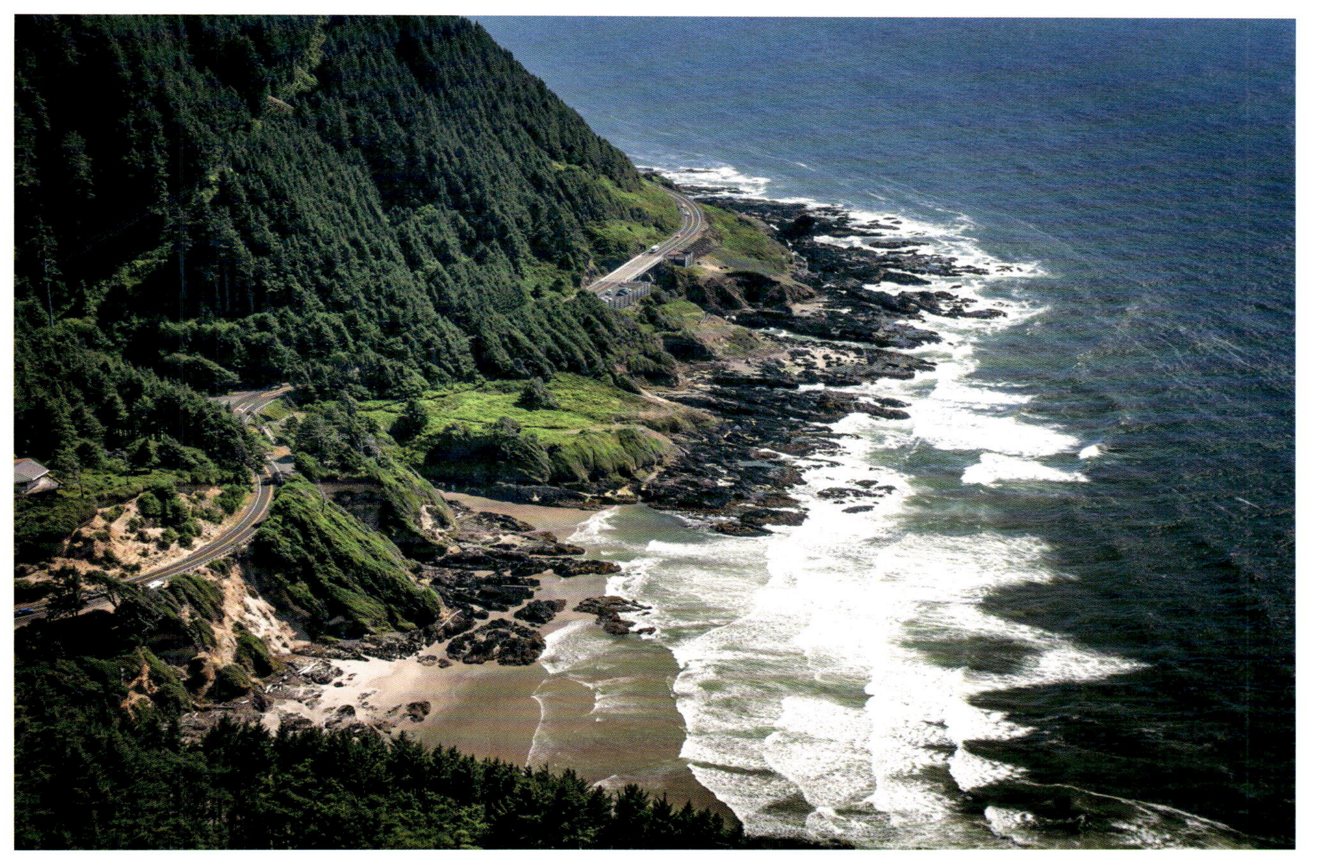

Cape Perpetua. *Photo by George F. Peterson.*   87

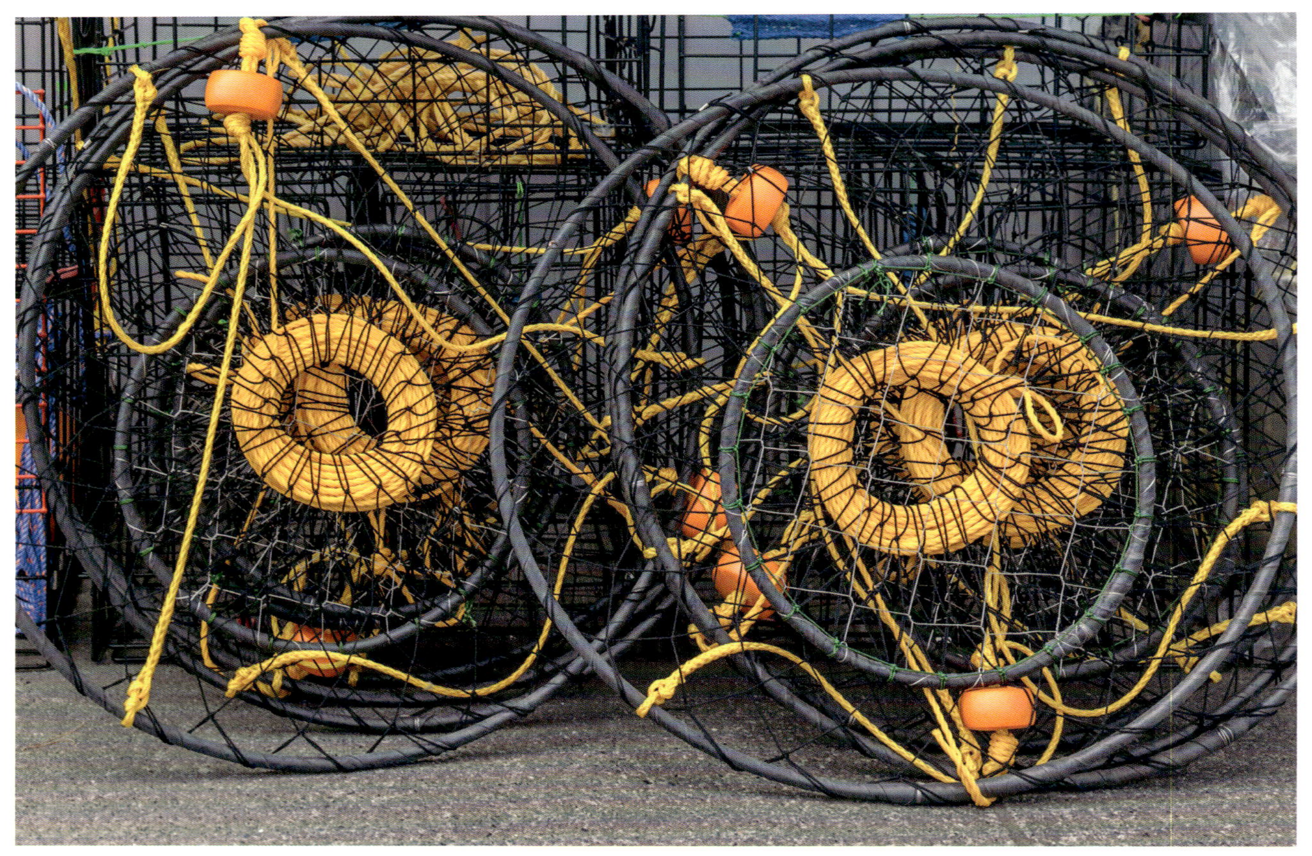

88　　Colorful crab nets. *Photo by Ellen Ahern.*

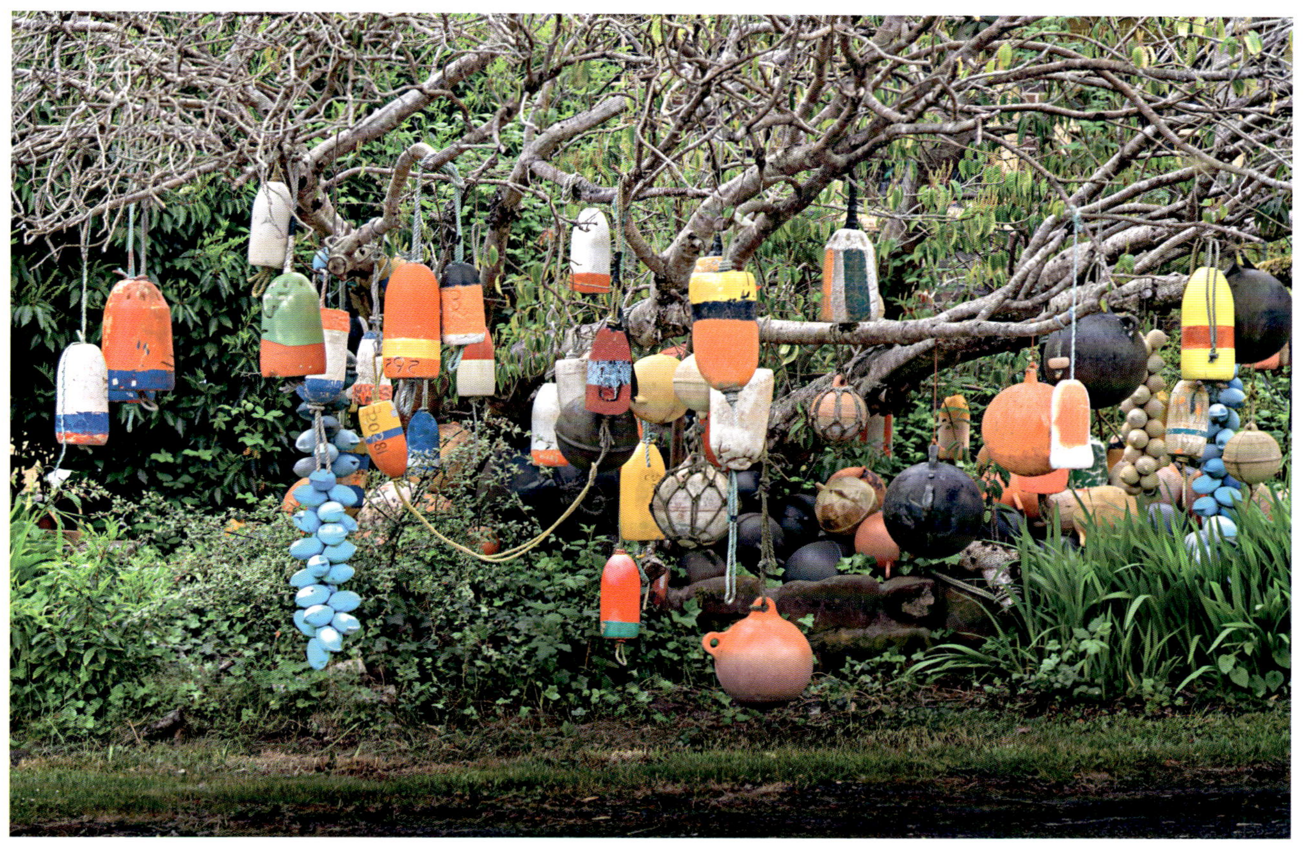

Buoy yard art. *Photo by Barbara Tricarico.* 89

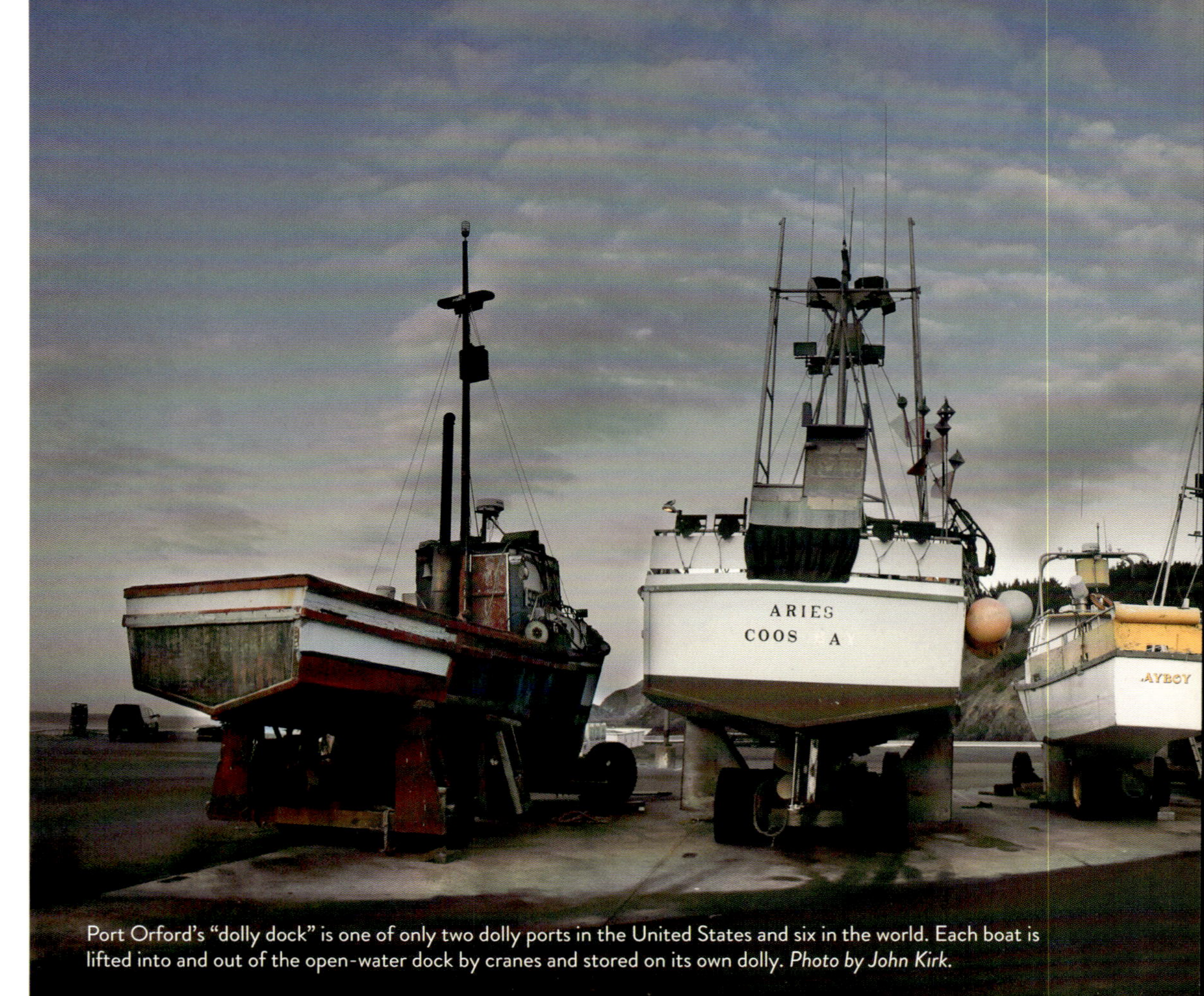

Port Orford's "dolly dock" is one of only two dolly ports in the United States and six in the world. Each boat is lifted into and out of the open-water dock by cranes and stored on its own dolly. *Photo by John Kirk.*

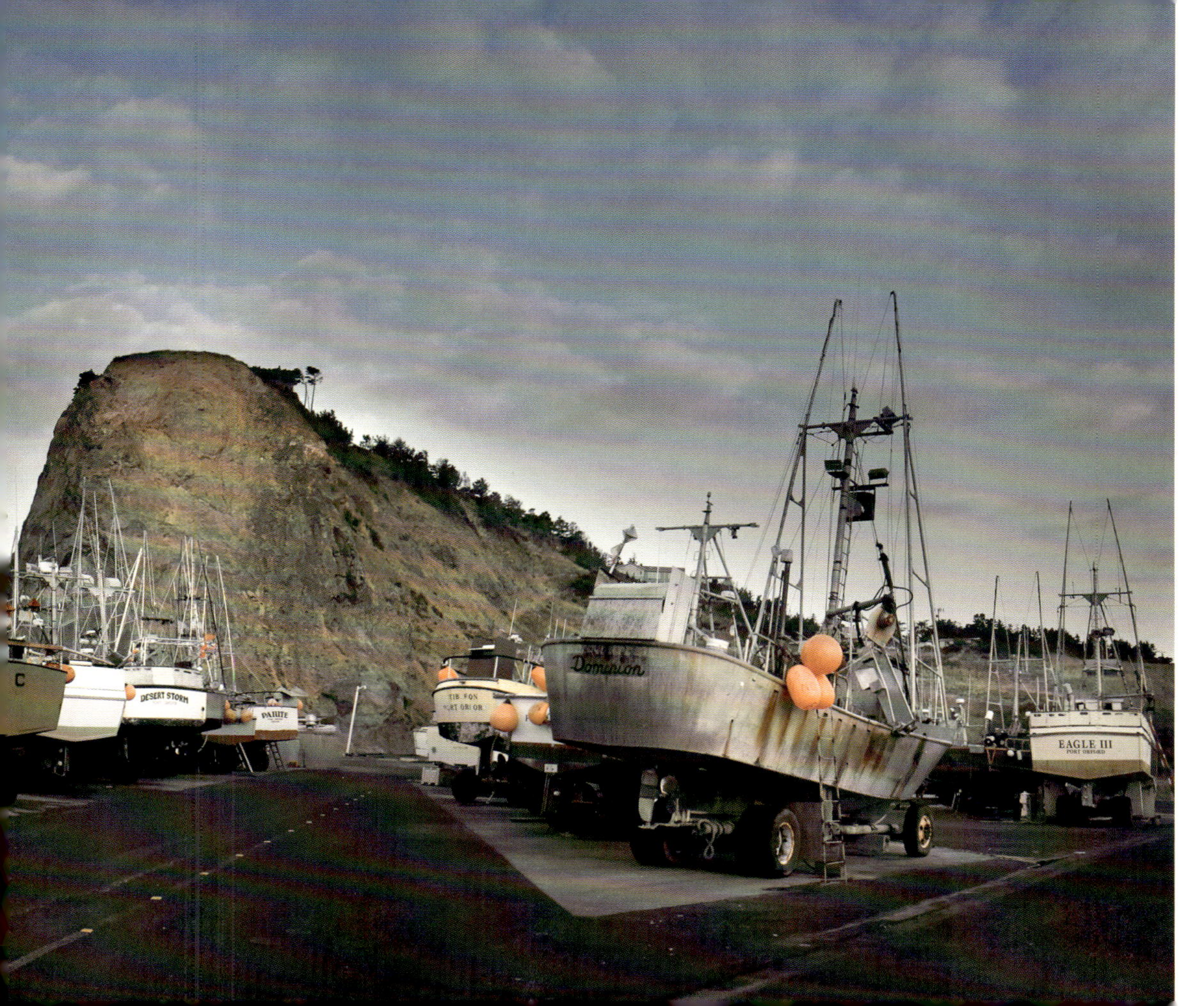
C
DESERT STORM
PAIUTE
TIB FON
PORT ORFORD
Domenion
EAGLE III
PORT ORFORD

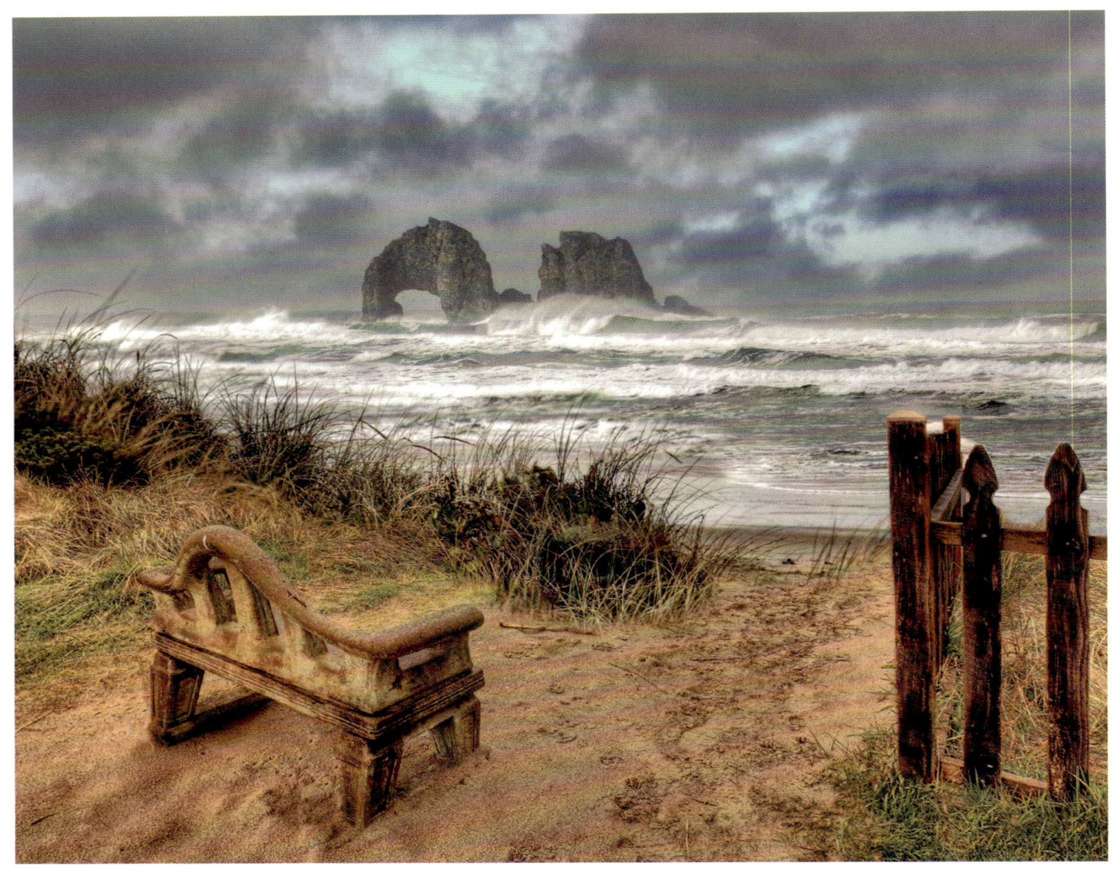

    The bench at Rockaway Beach. *Photo by Rudy Dierks.*

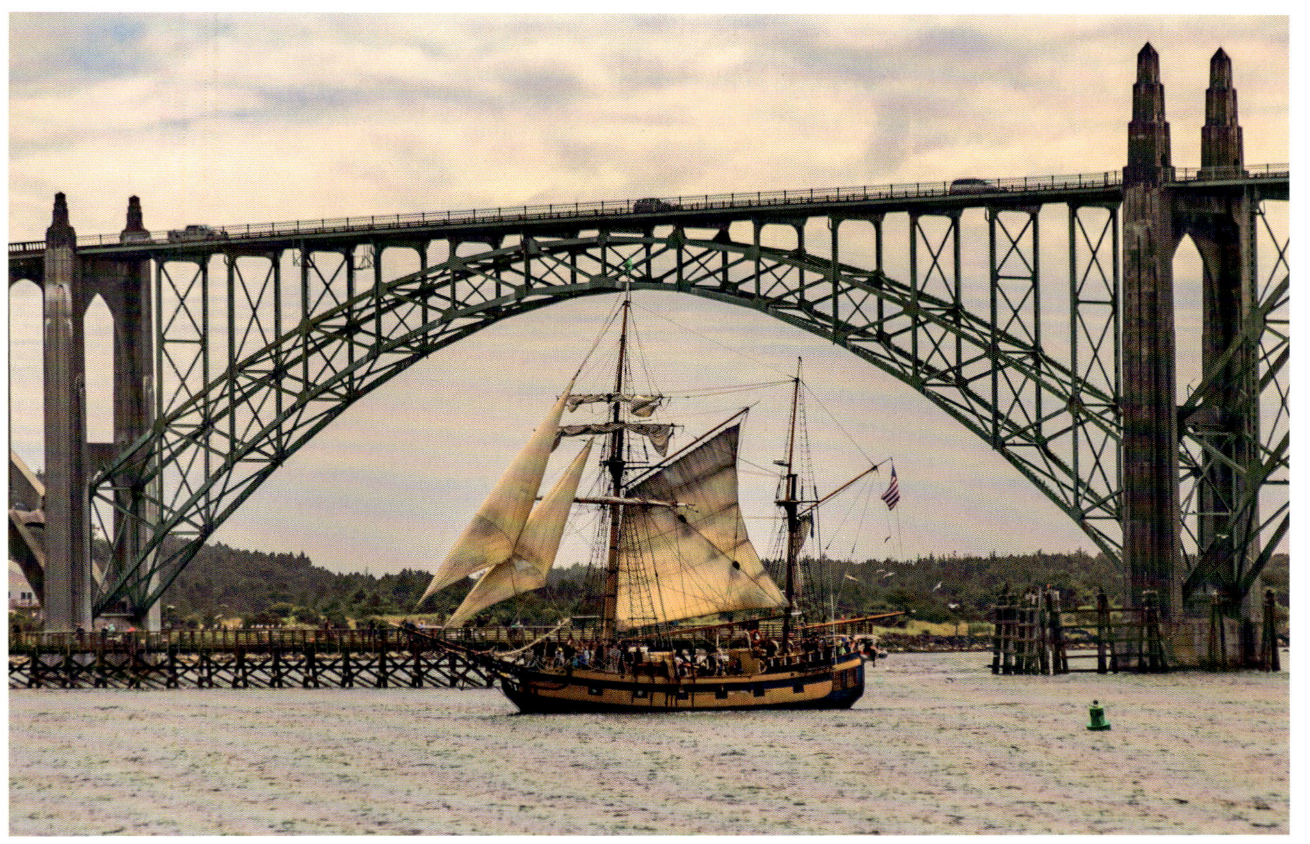

Tall ship at Yaquina Bay Bridge, Newport. *Photo by Vldn Taylor.*

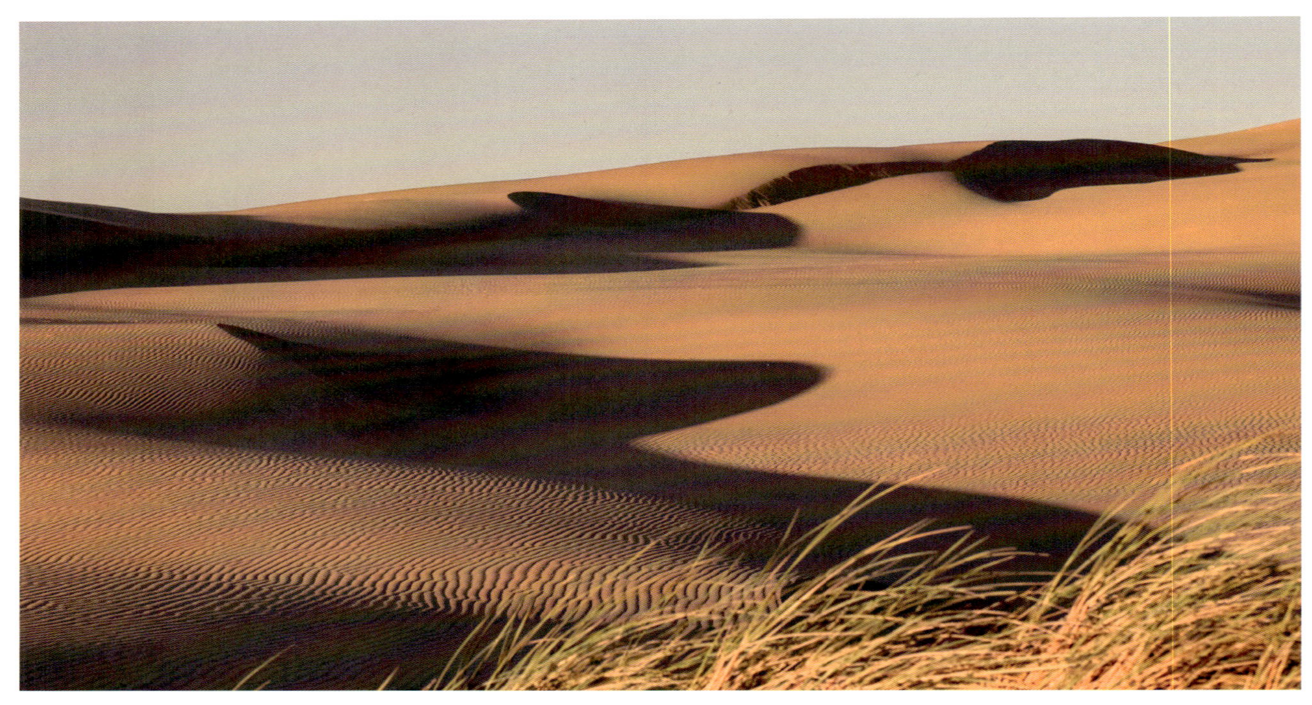

94   John Dellenback Dunes. *Photo by Vivian McAleavey.*

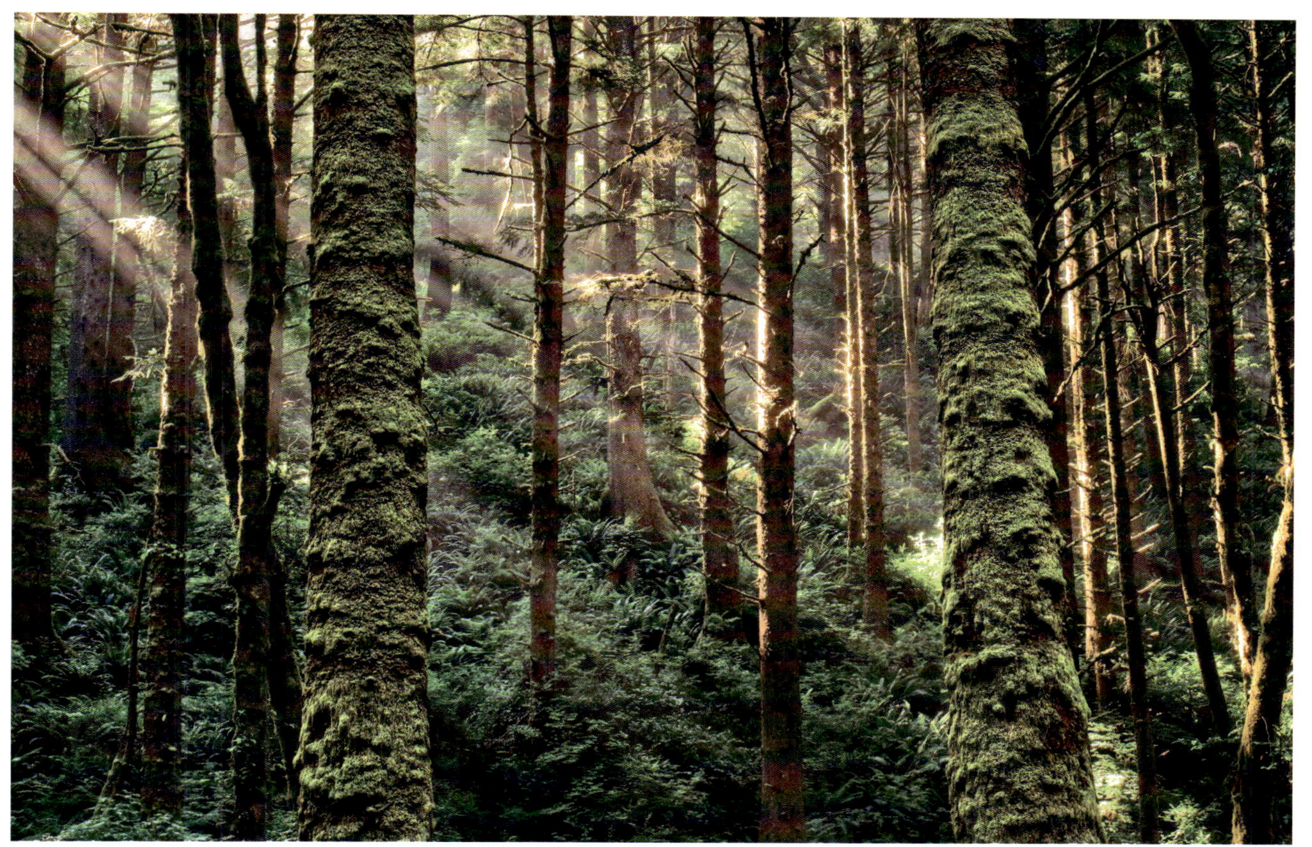

Rock Creek Campground, Florence. *Photo by Sue Newman.*   95

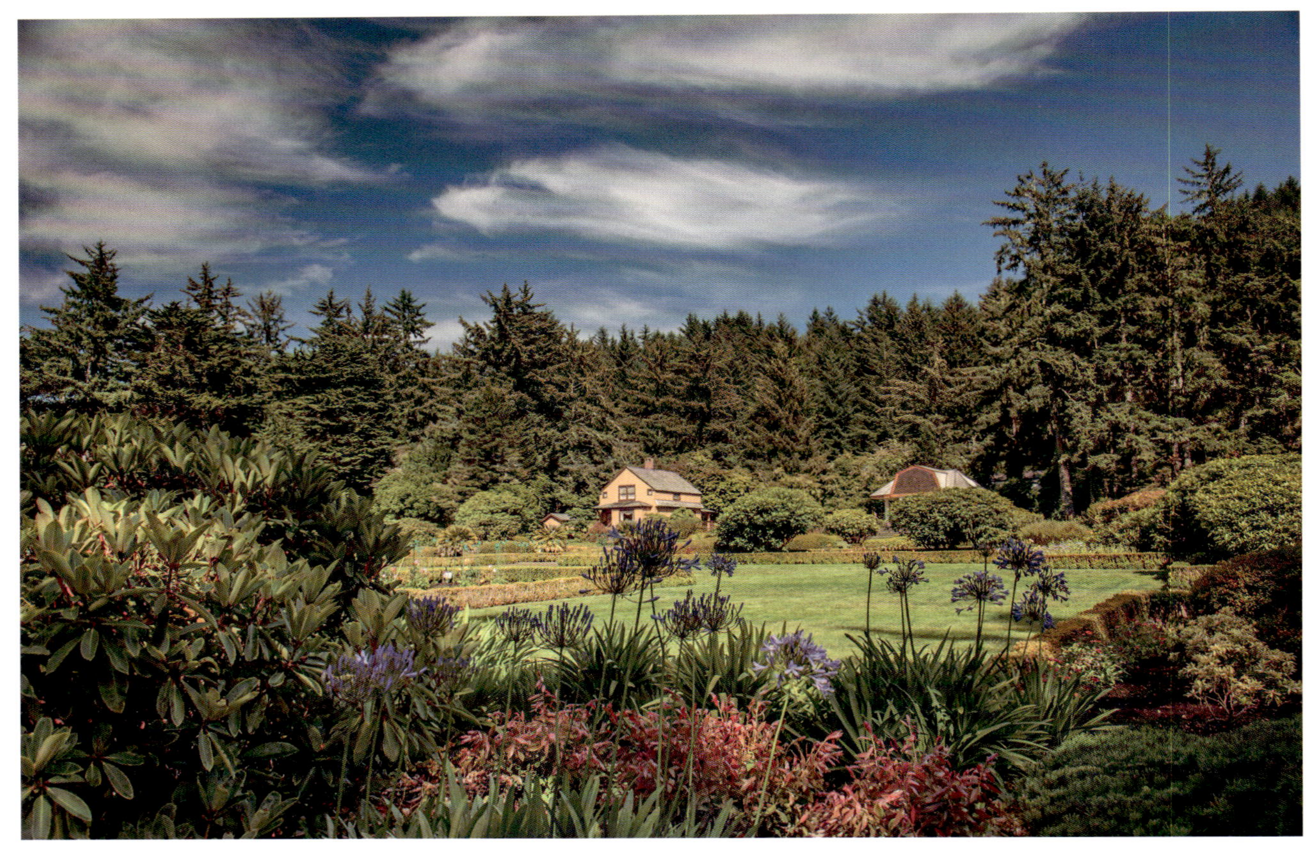

 Shore Acres State Park was once the private summer estate of shipbuilder and timber magnate Louis J. Simpson. *Photo by Ellen Ahern.*

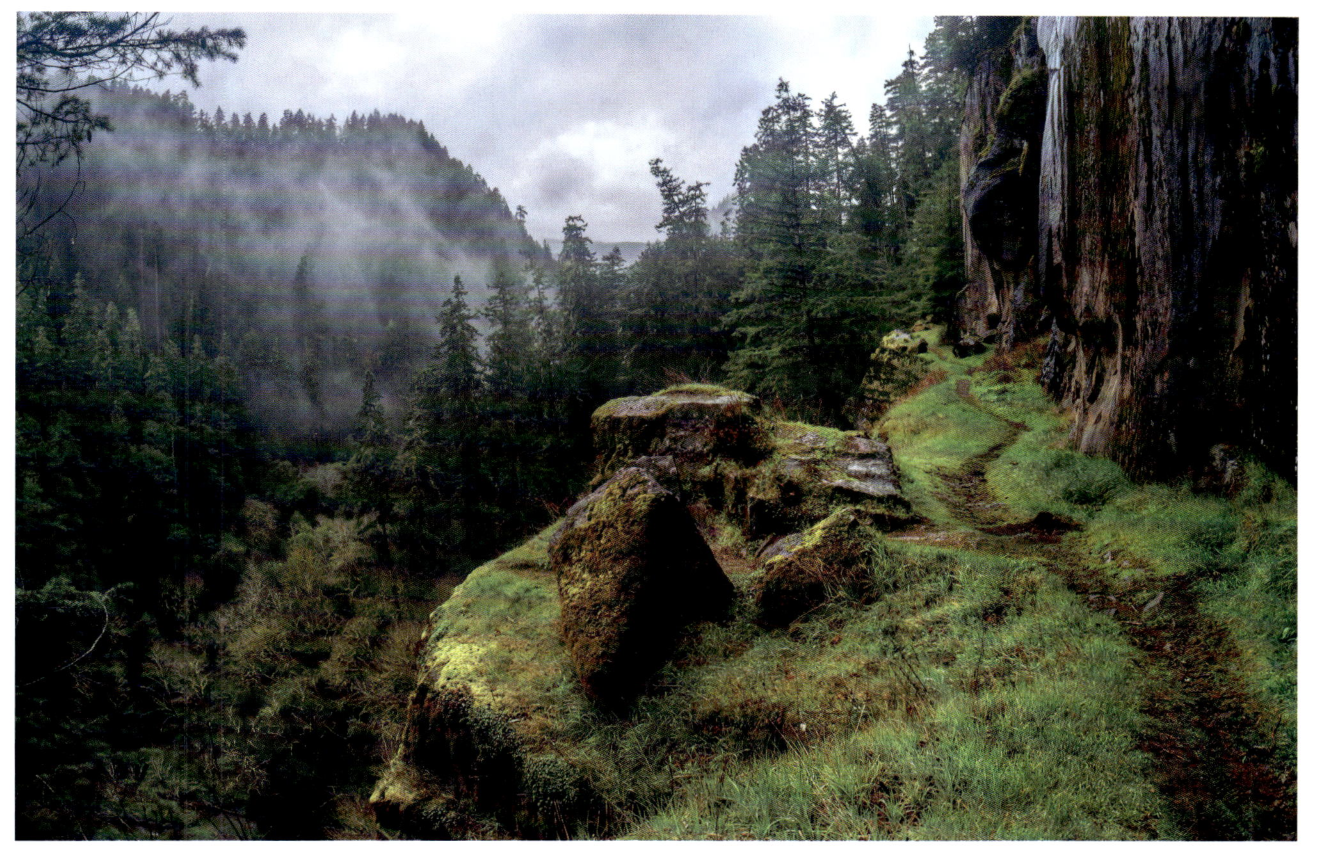

Golden and Silver Falls trail. *Photo by Sue Newman.*

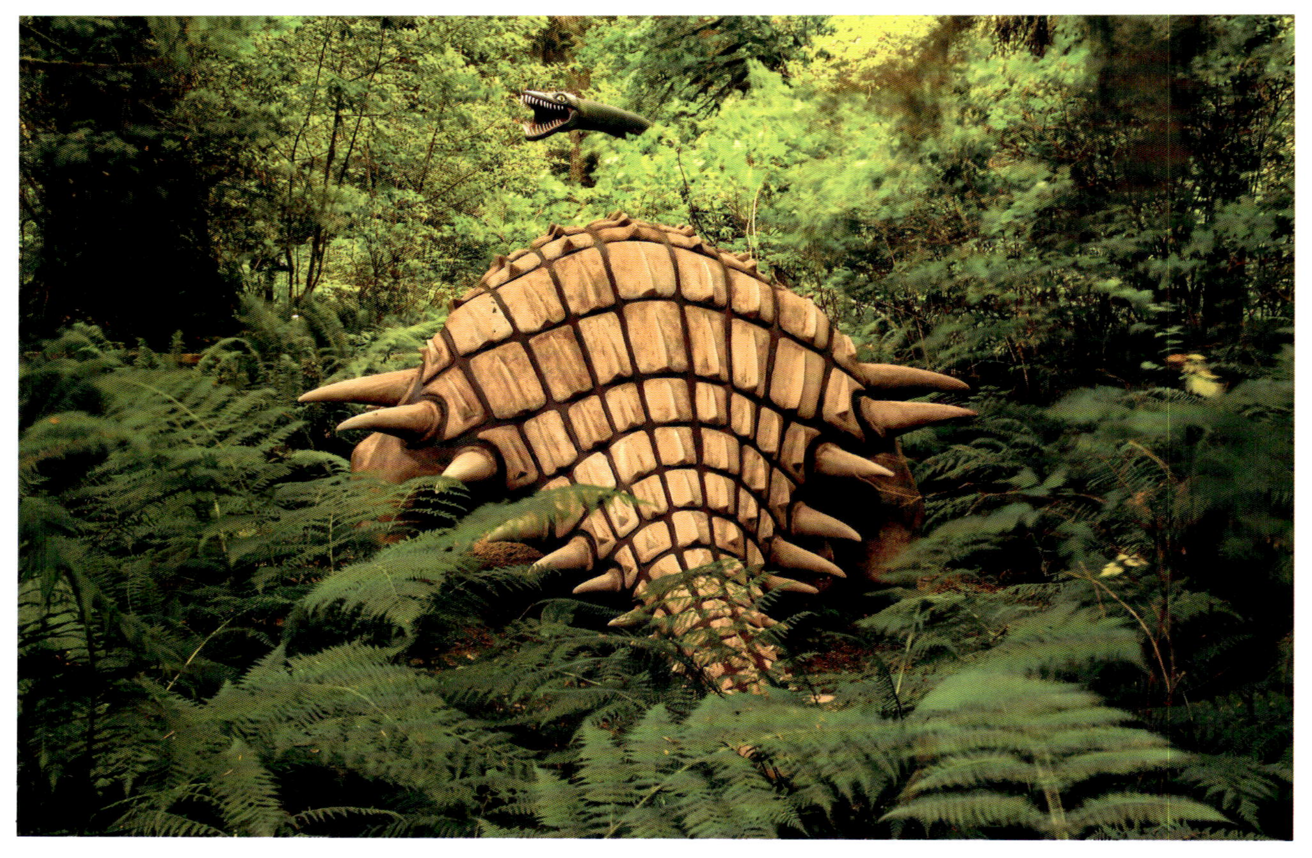

Prehistoric Gardens. Since 1955, this has been a popular roadside attraction along the Highway 101 coastal route near Port Orford. *Photo by Jay Newman.*

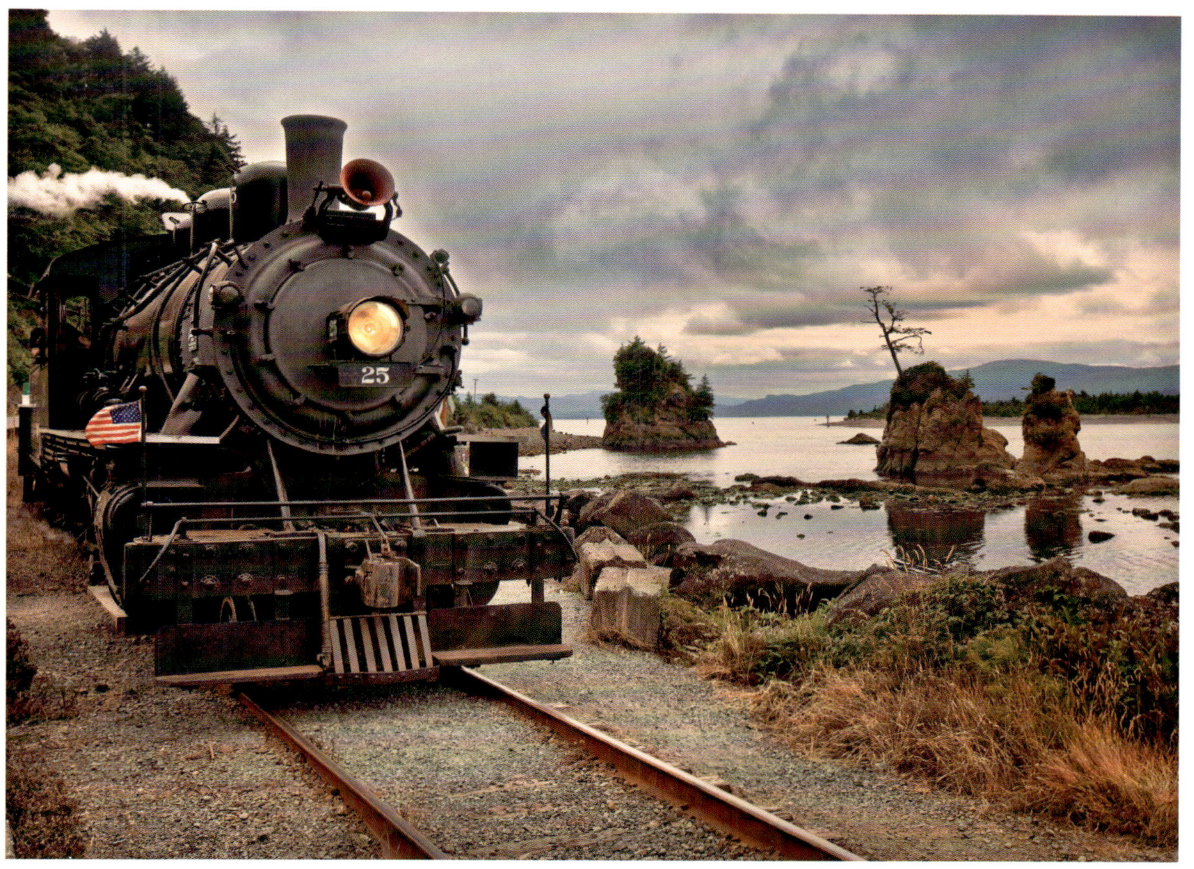

The Oregon Coast Scenic Railroad offers rides between Garibaldi and Rockaway Beach along Tillamook Bay. *Photo by Rudy Dierks.*

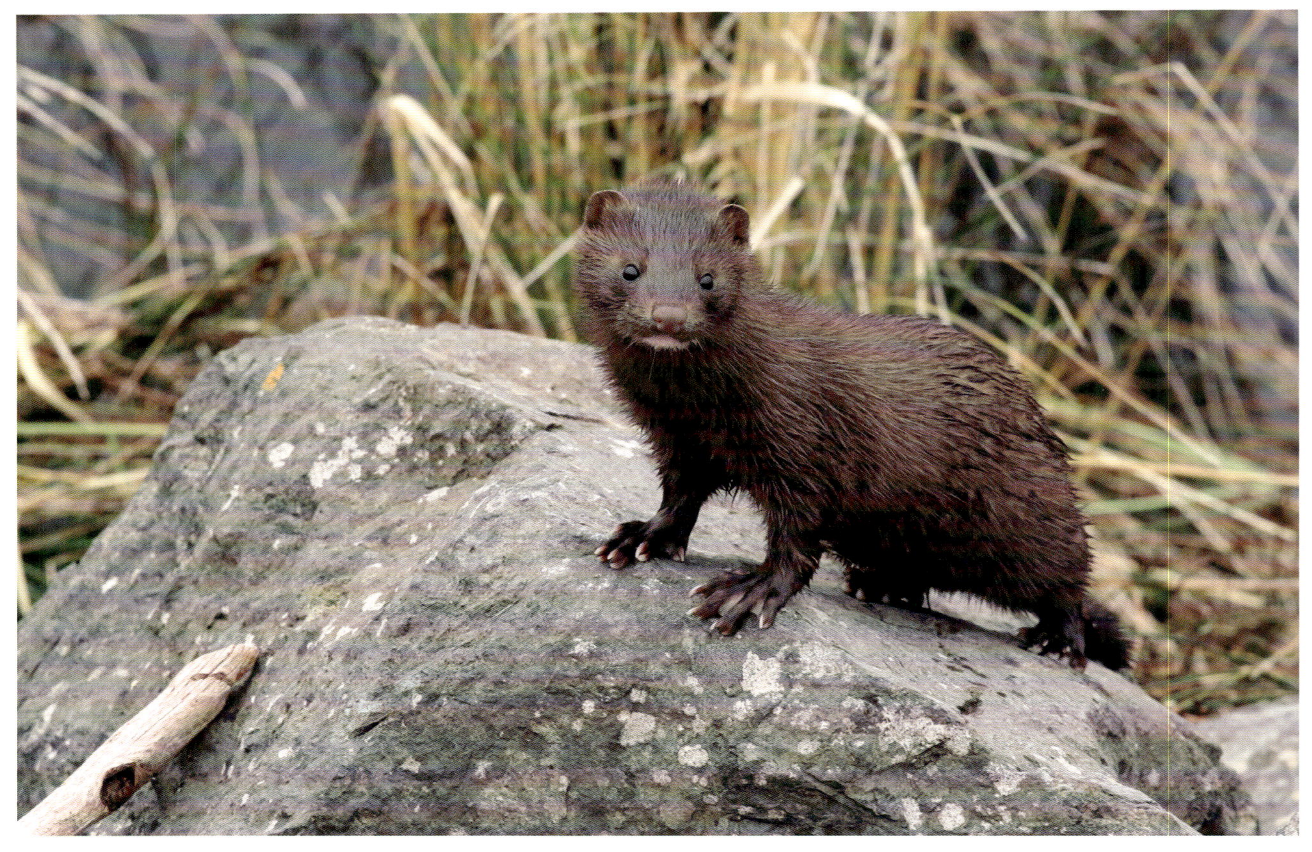

100   Mink. These small, semiaquatic animals are found throughout Oregon's rivers, lakes, and marshes. *Photo by Dan Elster.*

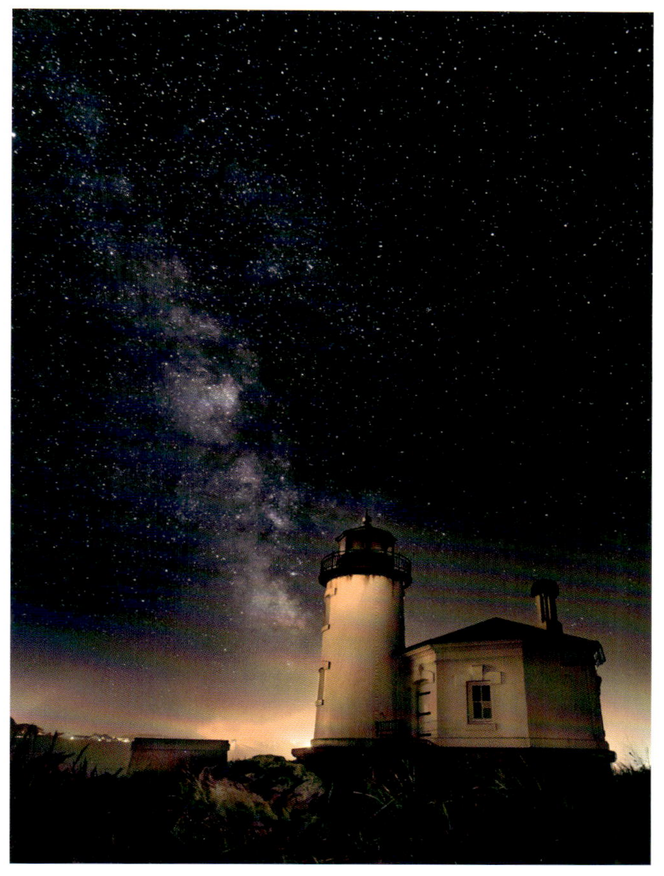

Milky Way above Coquille River Lighthouse, Bandon. *Photo by Linda Rodgers.* 101

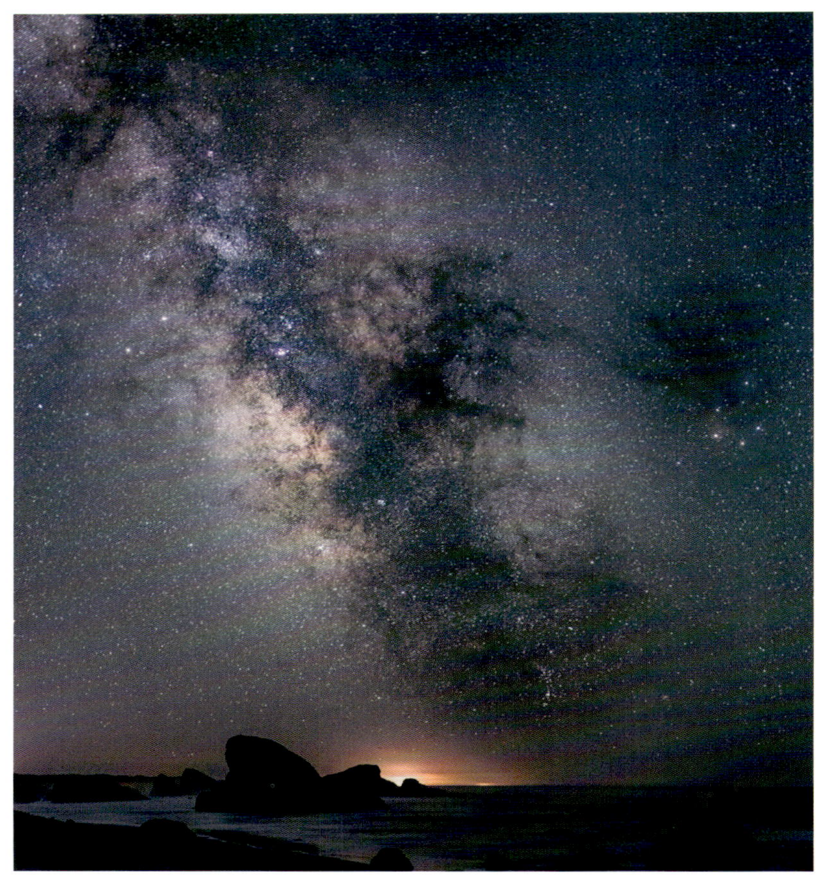

102   Milky Way above Myers Creek Beach, near Gold Beach. *Photo by Earshel Hogan.*

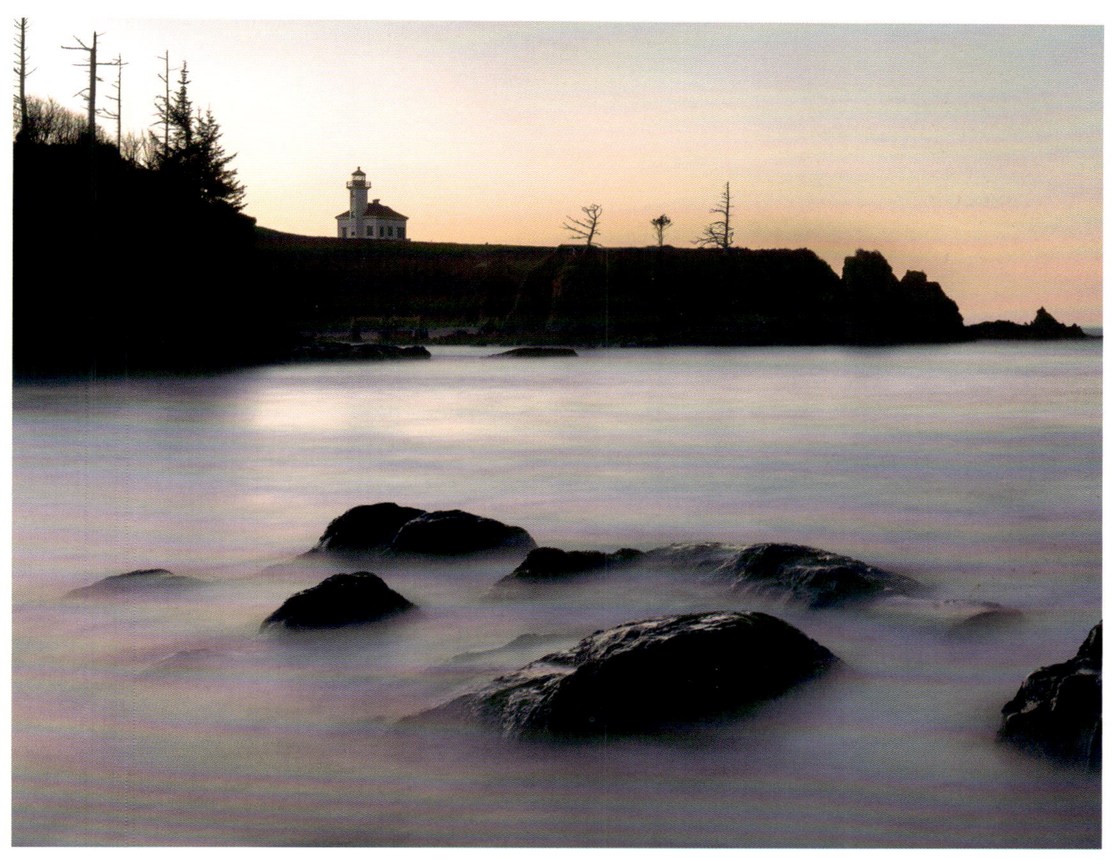

Cape Arago Lighthouse. In 1866, when Cape Arago's Fresnel lens was first lit,
Coos Bay was a busy shipping harbor for lumber and coal. *Photo by Vldn Taylor.*   103

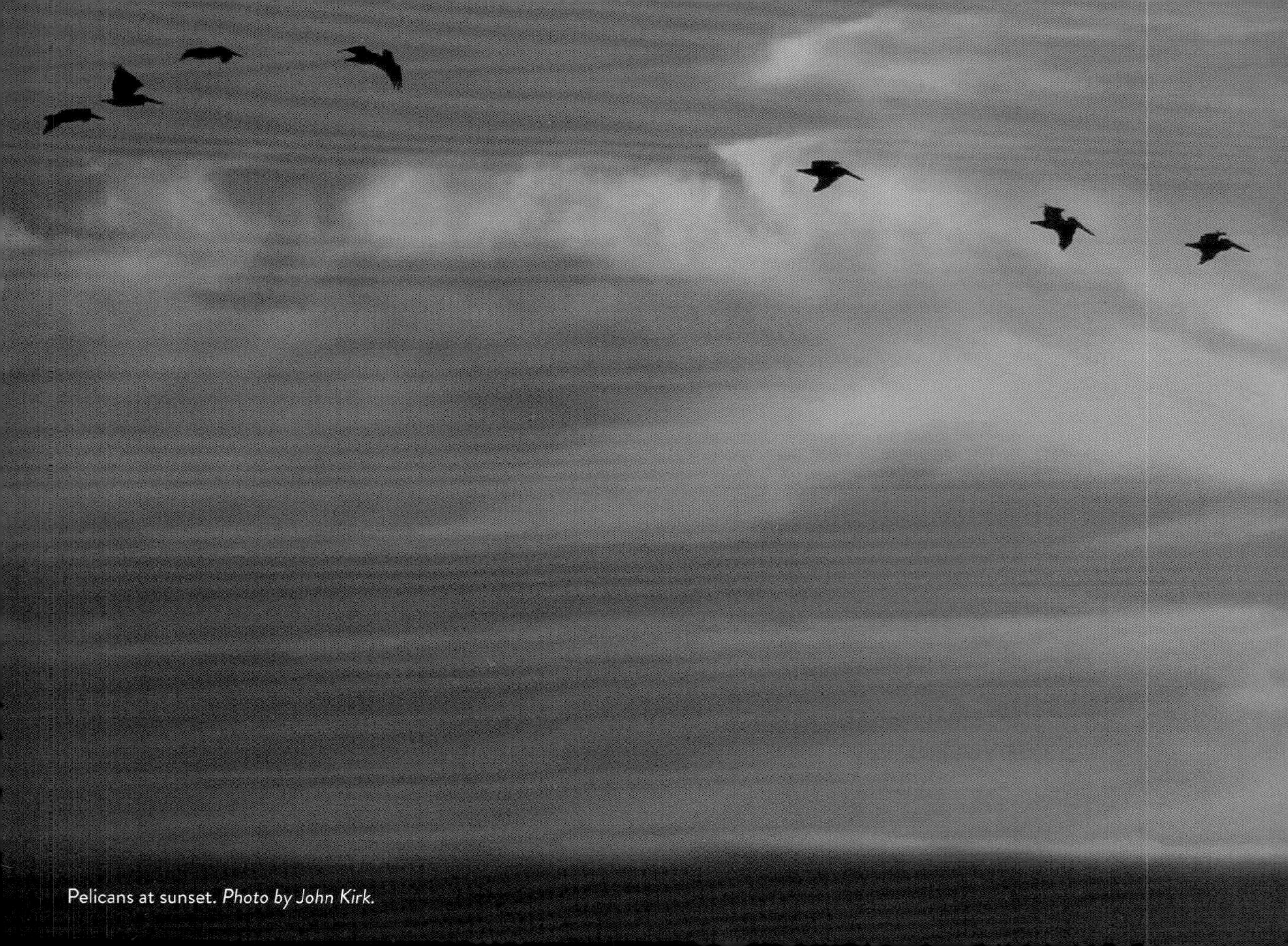

Pelicans at sunset. *Photo by John Kirk.*

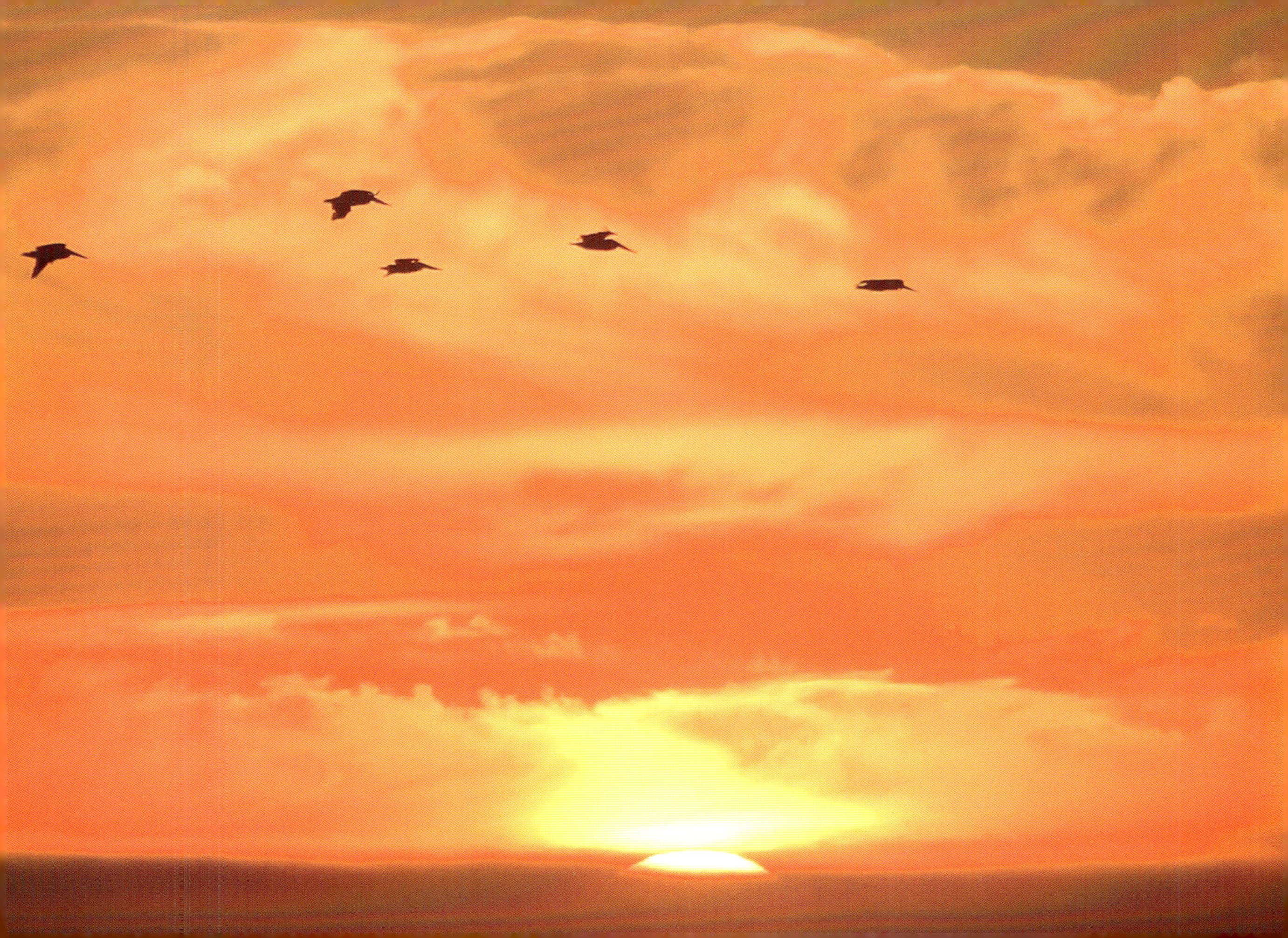

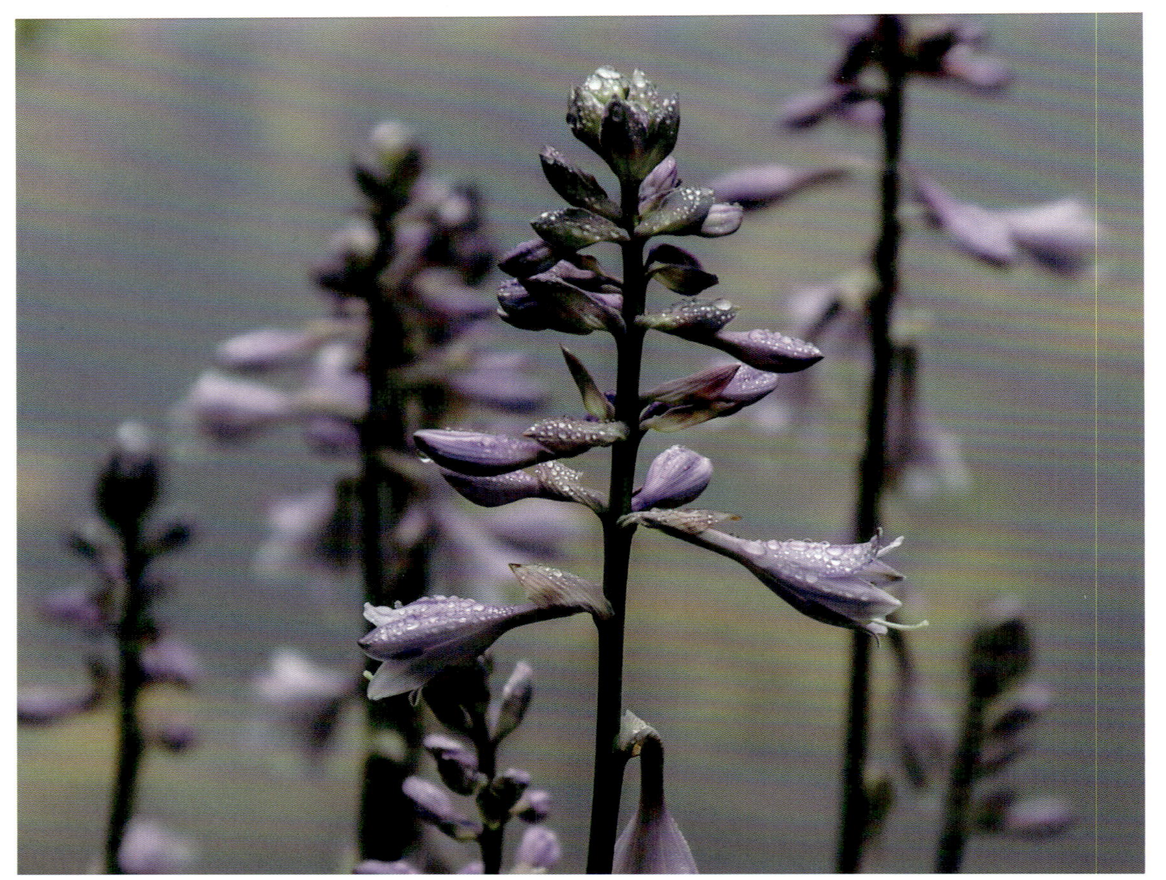

106   Hosta "Purple Heart" flowers. *Photo by George F. Peterson.*

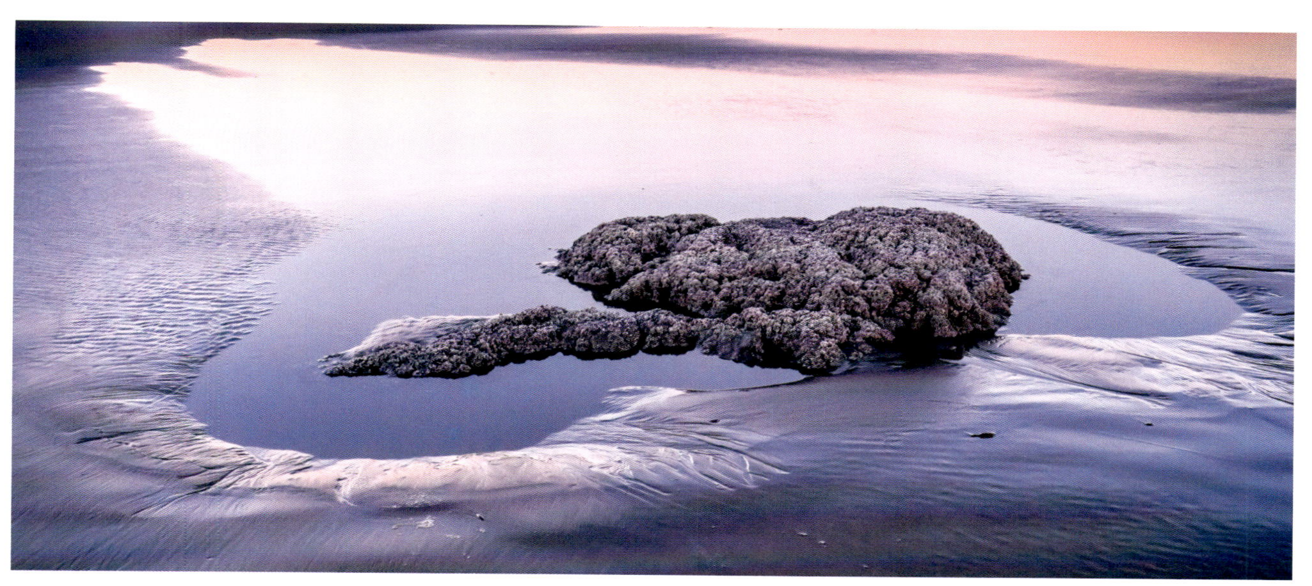

Bandon. *Photo by Kate Geary.*   107

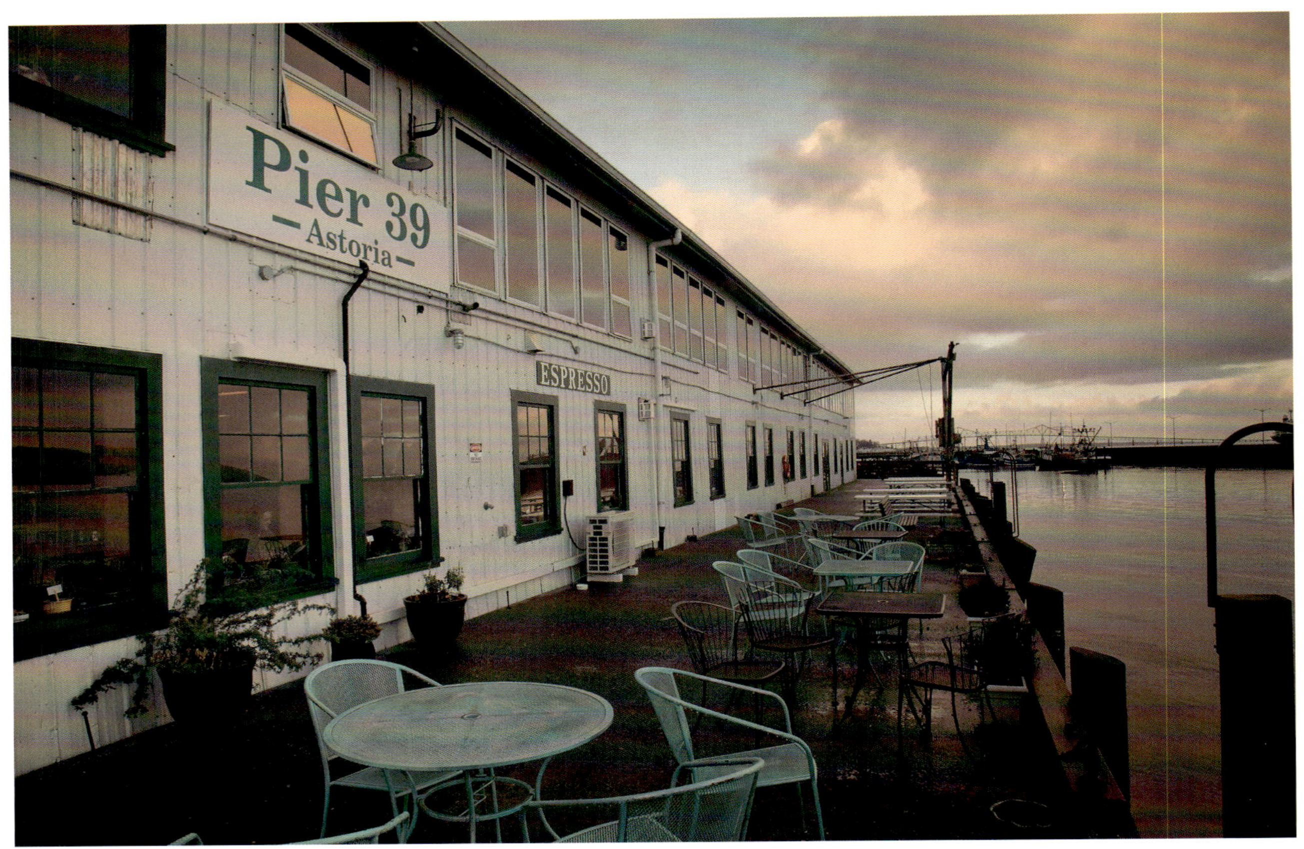

108   Dining over the Columbia River at Pier 39 in Astoria. *Photo by John Kirk.*

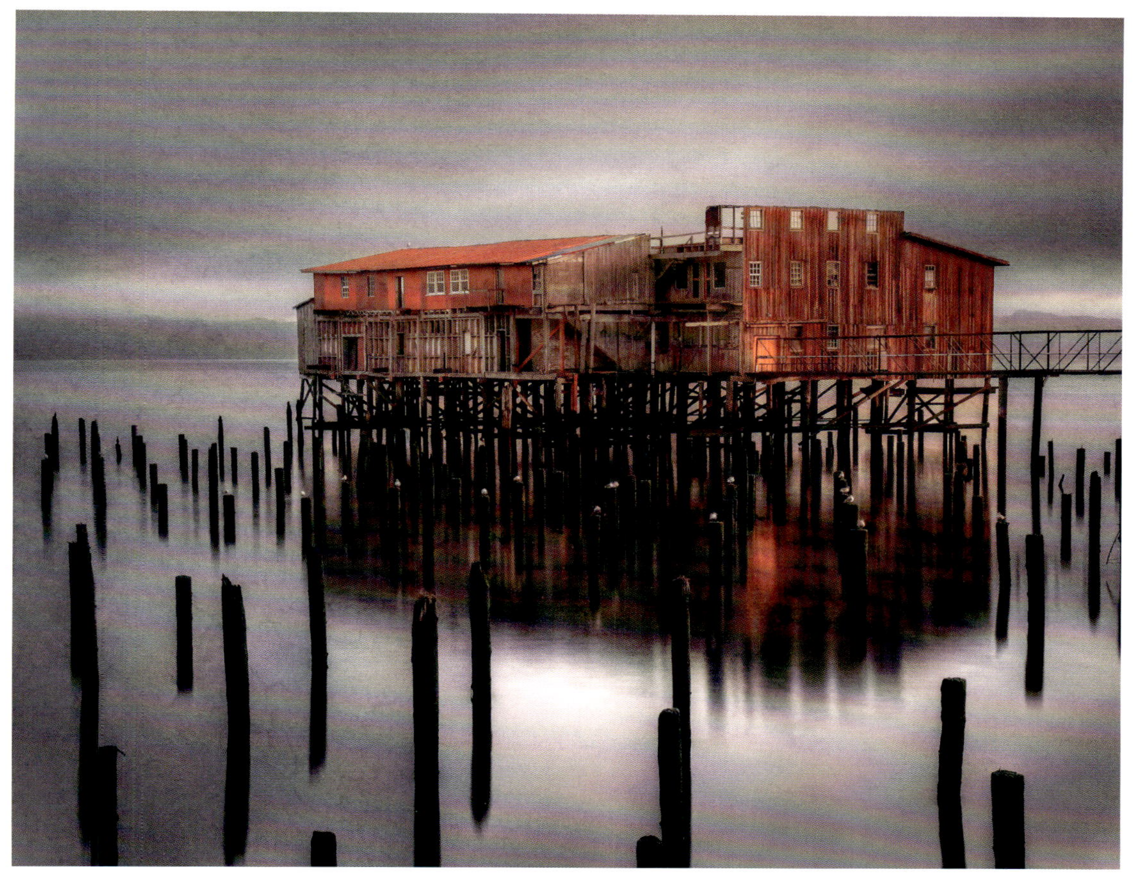

Old Cannery building, Astoria. *Photo by John Kirk.* 109

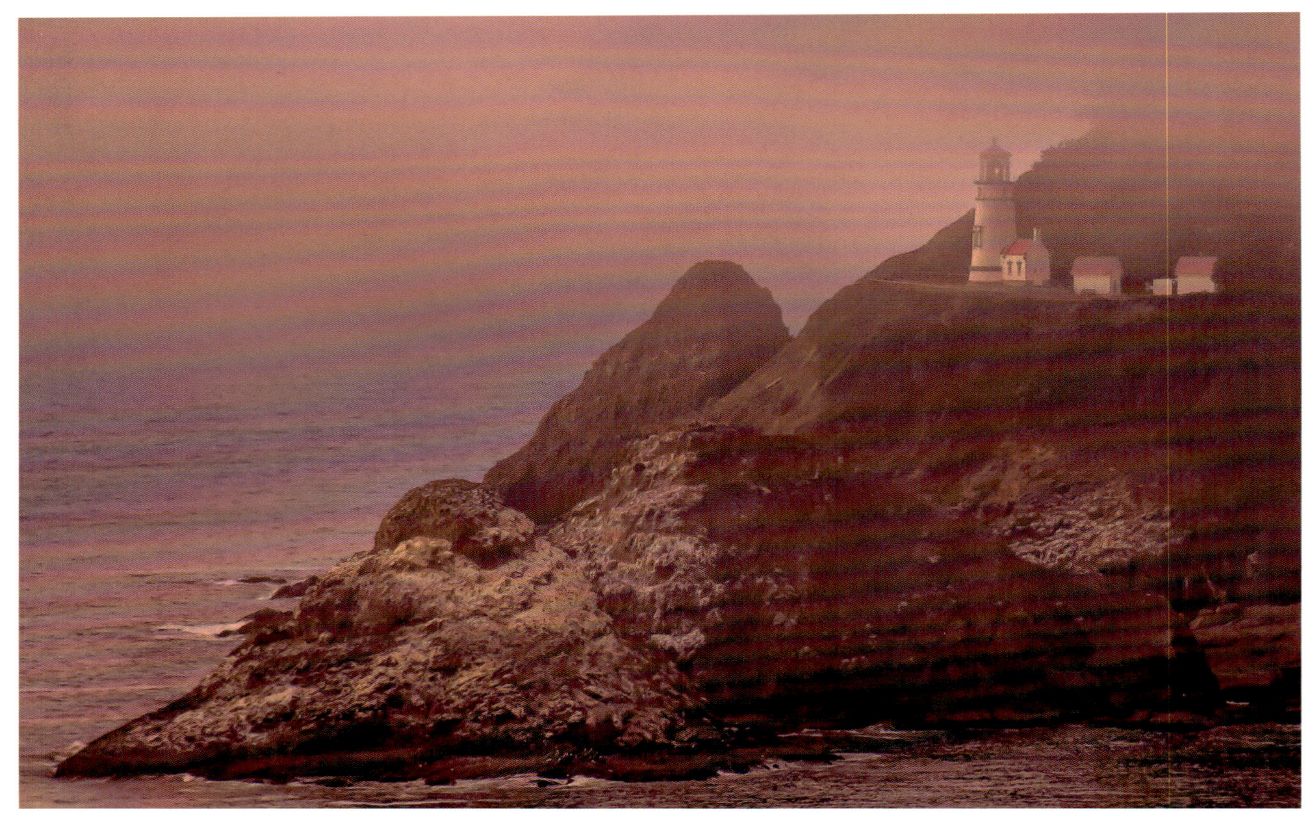

Heceta Head Lighthouse. The Oregon Parks and Recreation Department maintains the working lighthouse, and the lightkeeper's home is an interpretive center. The US Forest Service now operates the six assistant lightkeepers' homes as a bed and breakfast. *Photo by Clem Paslack.*

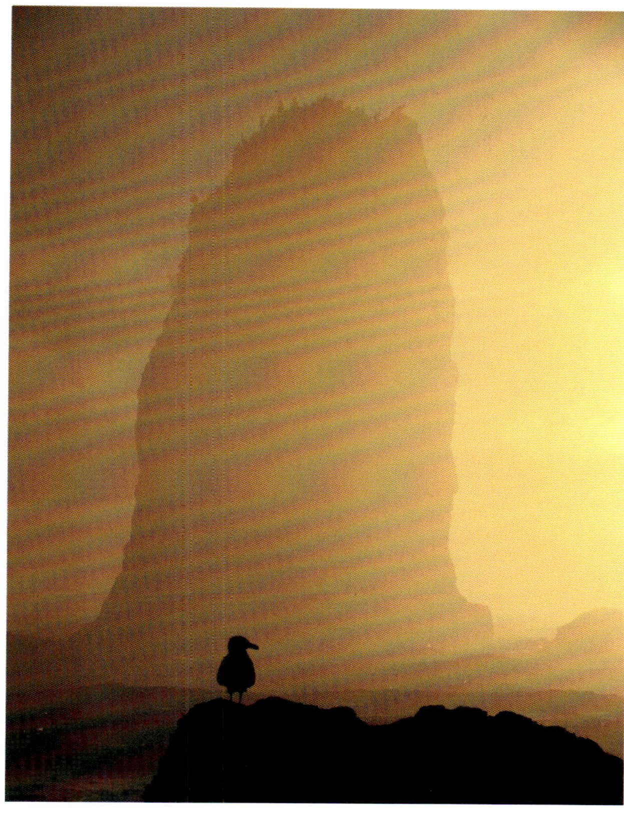

CREDITS

The following Oregon photographers contributed to this book.

Ellen Ahern	Graham Lewis
Ken Deveney	Mason Marsh
Marilyn Dierks	Vivian McAleavey
Rudy Dierks	Geri H. Mathewson
Dan Elster	Jay Newman
Doug Farrell	Sue Newman
Terry Fisher	Clem Paslack
Kate Geary	John Christer Petersen
Brandon Herring	George F. Peterson
Charles Hillestad	Linda Rodgers
Earshel Hogan	Sue Stendebach
Howard Hunt	Vldn Taylor
John Kirk	Neal R. Thompson
Richard Krieger	Barbara Tricarico
Judy Benson LaNier	David Lorenz Winston

The Needles, Cannon Beach. *Photo by Charles Hillestad.*   111

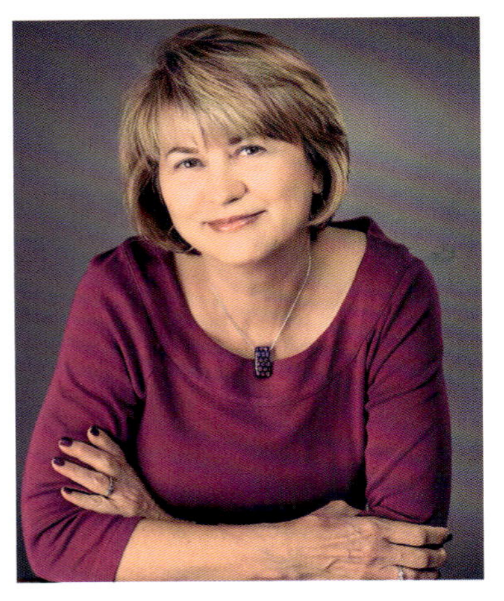

Barbara Tricarico has produced three coffee-table photography books by Schiffer Publishing: *Oregon*; *Ashland, Oregon;* and *Ashland, Oregon, Day Trips*, as well as coauthoring and photographing *Quilts of Virginia: 1607–1899*. She and her husband, Bill, moved to Ashland in 2010. Barbara is an active member of the Ashland Chamber of Commerce, is president of the Southern Oregon Photographic Association, and volunteers for the Ashland Food Project and the Oregon Shakespeare Festival. Barbara enjoys traveling and quilting. Follow her on Facebook at Barbara Tricarico Photography or visit her website, www.barbaratricarico.com.

Photo: Cornelius Matteo